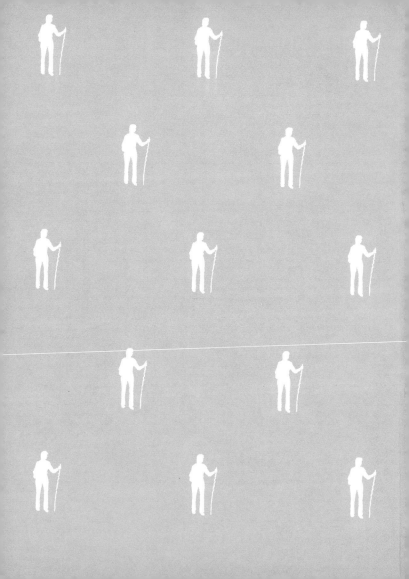

DAY HIKES
OF THE SMOKIES

TEXT BY
CARSON BREWER &
FRIENDS

GREAT SMOKY MOUNTAINS
ASSOCIATION
Gatlinburg, Tennessee

© 2002 by Great Smoky Mountains Association.

WRITTEN BY Carson Brewer, with supplemental text by Bill Beard, Woody Brinegar, Margaret Lynn Brown, Tom Condon, Donald E. Davis, Beth Giddens, Doris Gove, Ted Olson, Nye Simmons, & James Wedekind
EDITED BY: Steve Kemp & Coralie Bloom
EDITORIAL ASSISTANCE by Marianne Wightman & Jennifer Voorhis
DESIGN FORMAT BY: Christina Watkins
CARTOGRAPHY BY: International Mapping Associates, the National Park Service, and Bob Lochbaum
ELEVATION PROFILES BY: Joey Heath & Bob Lochbaum
PHOTOGRAPHY BY: Kent Cave, Mary Ann Kressig, Bill Lea, Nye Simmons, Scott Lamm, & Jerry Whaley
PRINTED IN THE U.S.A. ON RECYCLED PAPER BY LITHOGRAPHICS.

6   7   8   9

ISBN 0-937207-36-5

Great Smoky Mountains Association is a nonprofit organization which supports the educational, scientific, and historical programs of Great Smoky Mountains National Park. Our publications are an educational service intended to enhance the public's understanding and enjoyment of the national park. If you would like to know more about our publications, memberships, and projects, please contact: Great Smoky Mountains Association, 115 Park Headquarters Road, Gatlinburg, TN 37738 (865) 436-0120. www.SmokiesStore.org

CONTENTS

ACKNOWLEDGMENTS

I wish to express appreciation to the following who have been helpful in the preparation of this book:

Stanley G. Canter, former chief of interpretation for Great Smoky Mountains National Park; Ron Click, park technician; Glenn Cardwell, park technician; former chief naturalists Paul F. McCrary, Ross Bender and Neil P. Reid. And Arthur Stupka, biologist and former chief naturalist who contributed valuable information and suggestions for the original manuscript.

The Knoxville News-Sentinel, which printed the original stories from which some of the hikes are adapted.

-Carson Brewer

USING THIS GUIDE

MAPS . . . .

The grid coordinates (*e.g.* A1) on this book's MAP KEY corre-
spond to the grid on the official *Great Smoky Mountains Trail Map*
available for sale at park visitor centers. This excellent map
includes all official park trails, backcountry campsites, and regula-
tions. At least two commercial hiker's topographic maps
(Earthwalk Press and Trails Illustrated) also include the grid which
corresponds to our MAP KEY codes. They come in 1:62,500 scales
and paper or plastic versions. The United States Geological Survey
(USGS) maps referred to in the narratives are 1:24,000 scale (7.5
minute). All of these maps are available at park visitor centers or
by contacting GSMA at (865) 436-0120 or www.SmokiesStore.org

The trail profile charts which accompany each narrative were
designed to show how long and how rigorous each trail is and to
locate major landmarks and trail junctions. The diamond symbols
in these charts indicate unbridged stream crossings. The trail maps
which accompany each narrative have accurately shaded topogra-
phy and are designed at different scales to fit on one page. Trail
locations on these maps are based on recent GPS data and are
more accurate than quad maps. Mileages on trail maps generally
indicate distances between trail junctions.

Mileages, maps, and elevations are based on information provided by volunteer extraordinaire Bob Lochbaum, who meticulous-
ly measured each trail segment in the park at least twice. His distances and elevations are much more accurate than any information on park trails available in the past. It may take several years
for trail signs to reflect the new distances.

Each trail narrative begins with a callout section like the one shown below. An explanation of each component follows here.

> **LENGTH**: 10.0 miles, from Fontana Lake to Noland Divide Trail.
> **HIGHLIGHTS**: 6 backcountry campsites, fishing along the creek.
> **CAUTIONS**: 4 unbridged creek crossings.
> **MAP KEY**: 6-7 F-G; USGS quads: Noland Creek, Bryson City, Clingmans Dome.
> **USE**: Horse and hiking trail.
> **TRAILHEAD**: Drive 8.0 miles on Lakeview Drive northwest from Bryson City. Take the access trail from the parking lot at the bridge over Noland Creek.

LENGTH: Indicates the total mileage of the trail from the beginning and ending points listed. This book uses mileages recently obtained from a thorough remeasurement of all park trails. It is much more accurate than any other source for trail distances.

The length callout also shows which direction the narrative runs (*e.g.* from "Fontana Lake" to the junction with the "Noland Divide Trail.") Car shuttle recommended means the hike works best when a second car is placed at the end point.

HIGHLIGHTS: Some of the trail's more notable traits.

CAUTIONS: Potential hazards.

MAP KEY: The number and letter codes refer to the grids on the side of the official *Great Smoky Mountains Trail Map*. Topographic hiking maps produced by Earthwalk Press and Trails Illustrated use the same grid. The "USGS quads" refer to 7.5 minute (1:24,000 scale) topographic maps produced by the United States Geological Survey. Maps may be purchased at park visitor centers and other locations. To order Smokies quads from Great Smoky Mountains Association by phone, call (865) 436-0120.

USE: If listed simply as "Hiking trail" no horses are allowed.

TRAILHEAD: Directions to the beginning of the trail. In some cases there are more than one possible starting points.

SAFETY & MEDICAL CONCERNS

STREAM CROSSINGS & WATERFALLS—Heavy rains cause swollen streams that may be unsafe to ford. Do not cross a stream unless you are sure you can make it. Also, make sure your pack can be discarded quickly, wear shoes to protect your feet, use a stout stick for extra support, and, if you lose your footing, float with your feet downstream to protect your head. Just walking near a stream, on moss- and spray-covered rocks, can be hazardous. Waterfalls can be extremely hazardous; climbing on them has resulted in numerous fatalities.

DRINKING WATER—All water obtained in the backcountry should be treated before drinking to protect you from health hazards. The recommended treatment is boiling for one minute. Pump-style water filters may not remove certain bacteria or viruses but most now remove Giardia. Chemical disinfectants require very long contact times for the water temperatures found in the mountains. Do not drink untreated water! Even high elevation springs may be unsafe.

Waterborne illness can be spread by viruses, bacteria, and Giardia, all of which are undetectable by inspecting the water-source. Your first hint of problems may be cramps, diarrhea, nausea, or vomiting. Viruses or bacteria may affect you within 12-24 hours; Giardia's incubation period is 7-10 days, giving you time to get home before cramps and diarrhea strike. Treatment usually requires a physician's prescription, and sometimes extensive testing to reach a proper diagnosis.

BEARS & YOU—Black bears in the park are wild and their behavior is sometimes unpredictable. Although extremely rare, attacks on humans have occurred, inflicting serious injuries and death. Treat bear encounters with extreme caution and follow these guidelines:

If you see a bear, remain watchful. Do not approach it. If your presence causes the bear to change its behavior (stops feeding, changes its travel direction, watches you, etc.) YOU ARE TOO CLOSE. Being too close may promote aggressive behavior such as running toward you, making loud noises, or swatting the ground. The bear is demanding more space. Don't run, but slowly back away, watching the bear. Try to increase the distance between you and the bear. The bear will probably do the same.

If a bear persistently follows or approaches you without vocalizing or paw swatting, try changing your direction. If the bear continues to follow you, stand your ground. If the bear gets closer, talk loudly or shout at it. Act aggressively and try to intimidate the bear. Act together as a group if you have companions. Make yourselves look as large as possible (for example, move to higher ground). Throw non-food objects such as rocks at the bear. Use a deterrent such as a stout stick. Don't run and don't turn away from the bear. Don't leave food for the bear; this encourages further problems.

Most injuries from black bear attacks are minor and result from a bear attempting to get at people's food. If the bear's behavior indicates that it is after your food and you're physically attacked, separate yourself from the food and slowly back away.

If the bear shows no interest in your food and you're physically attacked, fight back aggressively with any available object—the bear may consider you as prey!

Help protect others. Report all bear incidents to a park ranger immediately. Above all, keep your distance from bears! Approaching any wild animal may disturb it. Wildlife harassment is punishable by fines of up to $5,000 and/or imprisonment for up to six months. To report a bear incident, call (865) 436-1230.

INSECT STINGS—Reactions to stings from yellowjackets, bees, and wasps range from minor local swelling to life threatening anaphylactic shock. Local pain and swelling are expected; in 24 hours the hand or foot may be swollen twice its size, and eyes may swell shut. The eye itself is not affected, only the eyelid, and vision is not in jeopardy. If stung on the hand, remove all rings immediately.

Though alarming, the condition will resolve in 2-5 days. Benadryl, an over-the-counter antihistamine, is helpful. Redness and local warmth are common, and not necessarily due to infection. Itching and hives (welts, like big mosquito bites) are a more serious reaction which should have medical attention promptly. Give Benadryl or other antihistamines immediately if available. Respiratory distress, wheezing, and/or collapse are potentially life threatening; antihistamines may help but injectable epinephrine in a sting kit is usually needed. Seek emergency medical treatment immediately.

Honey bees leave their stinger embedded in the victim, often with the venom sac still intact. Carefully scrape the stinger out with a credit card, pocket knife, or fingernail. Attempting to remove it with tweezers frequently squeezes the sac, injecting more venom into the victim.

Prevention requires prior knowledge of the allergy. Allergy shots to minimize the reaction need to be taken for a long time before being stung to be effective. Prescription sting kits should be carried by any sensitive individuals but are no substitute for desensitization. Many stinging insects are attracted to bright colors, perfumes, and moving objects. Try not to run if possible. You will likely be ignored, or investigated and left alone. However, if you have just stepped on or otherwise disturbed a nest, running may be the best choice. Multiple stings can make a person very ill without actual anaphylactic shock. In the United States, many more people die from insect stings than snake bites each year.

SNAKE BITES—There are Northern Copperheads and Timber Rattlesnakes within the park, but they are usually not aggressive, preferring to avoid human encounter. Most bites occur from stepping on an unnoticed snake, or when attempting to handle or play with the snake. Up to 22% of bites inject no venom. Prompt local pain and swelling signal injected venom, unless a rare bite directly into a vein has occurred.

Traditional field treatments using incision and suction, and constricting bands have been discontinued in the face of medical research. The word is slow to spread even among health professionals. Unskilled attempts at treatment often lead to severe complications, worse than the bite itself.

Keep the victim calm, avoiding any unnecessary activity. Splint the extremity as though for a fracture. Send for help. If walking out is necessary, do so slowly, and with frequent rest stops.

A tourniquet cuts off circulation, increases tissue damage, and may lead to amputation. Ice can cause extensive tissue damage when used on envenomated tissue, and increased circulation to the area will occur when the ice is removed.

Small children and the elderly are at greatest risk of serious injury, adults and older children may require hospitalization, but are seldom critical. Death is rare, and even without treatment is extremely unusual in the first 24 hours after the bite. Even though the Smokies receive 10 million visits per year, no fatality due to snake bite has ever been documented.

Avoid stepping over logs where a snake may be resting, and give any snake a wide berth. If you find yourself too close to a snake, avoid any sudden movement. A tongue darting at you is only the snake gathering scent to try to identify you, not a prelude to a strike. Don't put your hands where you can't see them when climbing or gathering firewood.

POISONOUS PLANTS—Learn to recognize poison ivy by its characteristic three leaf pattern. Vines may be difficult to identify, however, and any should be suspect. Playing or swinging on vines may be hazardous enough without adding the inconvenience of an itchy rash. Washing with soap and water within 30 minutes of exposure may be preventive; long sleeves and trousers will help. Smoke from burning poison ivy vines can cause the same rash, even inside of you, if breathed — don't throw vines on the fire.

BLISTERS—Prevention is much better than treatment. Two pairs of socks are preferable. The inner pair should be light and non-absorbent (not cotton), to prevent excess moisture buildup next to your skin. The outer should be wool or wool-synthetic blend for cushioning, and its ability to hold its loft when damp from sweat. The two socks dissipate friction by sliding on each other, rather than transmitting it to the skin surface. High tech socks that "wick" moisture away from the skin are expensive, but repay huge dividends in comfort.

Tape or moleskin any high friction "hot spots" that you are prone to before the hike. Band-Aids bunch up too easily to be effective. If you feel a "hot spot" developing, stop to add padding (tape, etc.) before the blister is fully formed. Once formed, a small blister may be covered in the same way. Larger blisters tend to tear open: cleanse the area well with soap and water, and drain with a flamed needle at the edge of the blister. Cover with tape. Keep the area clean to reduce the chance of infection.

ANKLE INJURIES—A twisted ankle can bring an outing to an abrupt halt. An audible snap usually signals a serious sprain (torn ligament) or fracture. Immediate first aid measures of ice may not be available and may be contrary to the goal of getting back to transportation at the trailhead. The decision to walk (limp) out or send for help is an individual one. If you can put weight on the ankle comfortably, then it is probably OK to walk out. The more one has to favor the ankle, the greater care must be taken. Don't lead with the injured foot, and pay special attention to foot placement. An assistant's feet may tangle with yours, resulting in another fall; use such help with caution. If excessive pain prevents weight bearing, determine if help is available. Taping is unlikely to help with the acute injury.

Those with weak ankles should favor heavy boots with adequate ankle support, and possibly a brace to wear in the boot. The slip-on variety sold in pharmacies and ace wraps offer no mechanical support; consult a physical therapist or orthopedic surgeon for the best available device, as well as strengthening exercises to reduce the chance of injury.

HEAT-RELATED ILLNESSES—Heat exhaustion is caused by water and salt depletion in a hot environment. Weakness, feeling faint, nausea with possible vomiting, headache, dizziness, and possibly fainting, alone or in some combination are frequent symptoms. Fever and confusion are usually absent. Muscle cramps may be present. The victim usually appears cool and clammy.

Heat stroke is a breakdown in the body's ability to regulate temperature. High fever, hot-dry skin (frequently but not always), and severe confusion or coma differentiate this life threatening condition from the milder heat exhaustion. Occasionally heat exhaustion symptoms precede heat stroke (20% of the time).

Prevention includes the use of cool, loose fitting clothing, frequent rest in a cool place, avoidance of direct sunlight, and drinking lots of fluids. Sweat losses of 2-3 quarts per hour are possible with exertion in hot surroundings. Certain drugs may affect sweat production or the way your body responds to heat stress. If it causes dry mouth, or blurred vision it may be a bad combination with heat; antihistamines should be avoided if possible. Check with your doctor ahead of time. High humidity further compromises your ability to stay cool. Drink enough fluid to maintain output of clear, dilute urine. Water is fine, or sports drinks diluted with water.

Field treatment for heat exhaustion consists of cooling measures: removal of excess clothing, seeking shade, lying down, resting, and oral hydration. Drink cool liquids slowly and steadily. Too much too fast may cause vomiting and make matters worse.

Victims of suspected heat stroke should be cooled at once by whatever means is available. Drenching the clothing with creek water would be ideal, but any water will do. Send for help. This is a true medical emergency.

LIGHTNING STRIKES—Lightning can cause mild injury as well as respiratory and cardiac arrest. Victims suffering respiratory or cardiac arrest may be saved through prompt bystander CPR with no medical equipment available. The heart usually starts again on its own after a brief period of inactivity. Breathing may take longer to recover; prolonged mouth to mouth assistance has led to successful recovery. Don't give up! Instruction in those techniques is not possible here, but regularly sponsored courses are available from your local Red Cross, American Heart Association, and many hospitals. Emergency medical evaluation is prudent for any survivor of a lightning strike; those who feel "OK" probably are, but should be checked as soon as possible.

Lightning was traditionally thought to seek the highest point for discharge, but is more complex in its behavior. Sometimes it hits where no predictive factors can be identified. It is most active around the edges of thunderstorms, and may strike before the storm seems to be upon you. Seek shelter away from solitary trees, high trees, rock outcroppings, or overhangs. It is thought to jump the gaps of overhangs much like a spark plug. It may travel down tree trunks and "splatter," and may follow wire fence lines. If no shelter is available, crouch in a shallow depression, away from any conductive material, or streams of water.

HYPOTHERMIA—This is an extremely dangerous condition involving the lowering of the "core" temperature (the temperature of the body's vital internal organs) beyond the lower level of efficient metabolic function. This causes involuntary shivering in an attempt to generate heat by muscular activity. At this point the victim may say they "feel very cold," but be rational. Confusion and loss of muscular coordination soon follow without treatment. One of the first signs may be a companion falling behind or tripping often. The victim may behave and walk as though drunk, and may lose coordination of fine motor skills such as those needed to strike a match. With this or soon after comes mental confusion, sometimes accompanied by seemingly irrational behavior. Hypothermic victims may be so confused as to undress in freezing conditions, or hallucinate—and act upon that hallucination!

Hypothermia (or exposure) is brought about by a combination of factors. Cold, wet, and wind are a potentially deadly combination even with temperatures in the 50s F. if you aren't properly prepared. Children, because of their greater ratio of surface area to weight, are especially vulnerable. At higher elevations in the park, there is a year-round potential for this to occur.

You lose heat through breathing, becoming wet, being exposed to wind, sitting on cold objects, and through radiant losses — the heat your body gives up to its surroundings. Prevention is aimed at those factors present on the day of your hike. Cotton is great for coolness in summer, but a disaster when wet and cold. Avoid blue jeans in the winter. Synthetic pile fabrics are best for dependable warmth. A wind and rain suit will do double duty in foul weather, offering added insulation against radiant losses. Avoid sitting on cold rocks or ground, and if possible breathe through a scarf or collar if you think you are getting in trouble. Be sure your head is covered as up to 40% of your heat loss can be from your head. In the winter, and transition seasons, take a sweater in case the weather turns, or you're caught out late.

Field treatment involves stopping further heat loss and warming the victim. Usually getting dry and warming with a hot drink are sufficient. More severe cases may require construction of an emergency shelter to warm the victim, but that is beyond the scope of this section.

PREVENTION—Many outdoor emergencies and too frequent fatalities arise from hikers ignoring basic park guidelines and common sense. Regardless of how small or large your group, tell a responsible person about your trip, and establish a check-in procedure. This person notifies park authorities if you are overdue. Keep your group together, and if a large group, designate a "sweep" person who will bring up the rear. No one falls behind this person. Pair off into a "buddy system," and keep track of your buddy. Stay on the trail. You won't be lost if you do, just "bewildered" for a bit. Get off the trail, and you can become truly lost in short order in the dense growth. You are then almost impossible to find from the trail — and the trails get searched first. If night finds you, stay put. The chance of injury and becoming more lost increase dramatically if you continue to wander. Do not "hunker down" right next to a noisy stream, you will be unable to hear the calls of rescuers.

Hiking alone is dangerous; if you must do so, leave a detailed itinerary with someone, and then stick to it.

Take appropriate clothing with you in a rucksack. Rain gear is always necessary. An emergency space blanket is no larger than your fist until needed and weighs only a couple of ounces. A coach's whistle can be carried in your pocket or around your neck, is audible from far away, and may be used long after you have yelled yourself hoarse. All children should have one; kids can become lost on a "nature break." Waterproofed matches in a water-proof matchbox should be in the pockets of any outdoor traveler. Fires in undesignated sites are strongly discouraged, but may be needed in a crisis.

GETTING HELP—If you are faced with a situation where out-side help is needed, don't panic. Take a few minutes to sit down and fully assess the situation and plan your actions. If possible, write down your location, the victim's name, and the suspected nature of the problem. In the heat of the moment, such essential information is often lost or confused. Also, this will help you focus clearly on the problems at hand. Plan your route to the nearest trailhead where help may be obtained, or back to your car as the situation dictates. Other passing hikers, or backpackers at back-country sites may be of assistance. Seek the closest phone or ranger station. The general information number is 865-436-1200. 911 emergency service is also available in many areas.

With a little common sense and good judgment, the chances of your having anything but fun are remote. Proper planning will fur-ther reduce the likelihood of problems on your outing.

Safety and Health Concerns courtesy Dr. Nye Simmons and the National Park Service.

PARKING & TRAILHEADS

The majority of trailheads are not indicated with prominent road-side signs. Be sure to follow the directions in this guide carefully to find the proper parking area.

The amount of parking available at trailheads is highly variable. Often the parking areas for the most popular trails fill by mid-morning during the busy season. If you find your intended trailhead is full, consider it an opportunity to seek out one of the park's many, many lightly used trails.

Theft from parked cars is a perennial problem in most national parks. Thieves almost always target purses, cameras, laptop computers, portable stereos, and other easily exchangeable commodities. The best defense is to keep valuables on your person. Locking them out of sight in your trunk may be effective, but then again most trunks are also easily broken into. Be aware that thieves may be in the parking area watching as you slip your purse into the glove box or stow your video camera in the trunk. Do not leave a note on your dashboard saying how long you will be hiking. Notify park rangers by calling (865) 436-1294 or 436-1230 to report a theft or suspicious activity.

SMOKY MOUNTAIN WEATHER

Local weather forecasts are posted at park visitor centers. Forecasts for longer than 48 hours hence are generally not reliable.

SPRING—March has the most changeable weather; snow can fall on any day, especially at the higher elevations. "Spring break" backpackers are often caught unprepared when a sunny day in the 70s F. is followed by a wet, bitterly cold one. Major blizzards have occurred as late as early April. By mid- to late April, the weather is usually milder.

SUMMER—By mid-June, heat, haze, and humidity are the norm. Most precipitation occurs as afternoon thundershowers. Summer weather generally persists through mid-September. At the lower elevations, expect highs in the mid-80s and lows around 60°. Above 5,000 feet, the highs will be in the mid-60s and lows in the low 50s.

AUTUMN—In mid-September, a pattern of warm, sunny days and crisp, clear nights often begins. However, cool, rainy days also

TEMPERATURES (F.) & PRECIPITATION (inches)

	Gatlinburg, TN, elev. 1,462'			Clingmans Dome, elev. 6,643'		
	Avg. High	Low	Precip.	Avg. High	Low	Precip.
Jan.	51°	28°	4.8"	35°	19°	7.0"
Feb.	54°	29°	4.8"	35°	18°	8.2"
March	61°	34°	5.3"	39°	24°	8.2"
April	71°	42°	4.5"	49°	34°	6.5"
May	79°	50°	4.5"	57°	43°	6.0"
June	86°	58°	5.2"	63°	49°	6.9"
July	88°	59°	5.7"	65°	53°	8.3"
August	87°	60°	5.3"	64°	52°	6.8"
Sept.	83°	55°	3.0"	60°	47°	5.1"
Oct.	73°	43°	3.1"	53°	38°	5.4"
Nov.	61°	33°	3.4"	42°	28°	6.4"
Dec.	52°	28°	4.5"	37°	21°	7.3"

occur. Most leaves have fallen in the high country by mid-October. The peak of fall color in the lowlands is late October. Dustings of snow may fall at the higher elevations in November.

WINTER—Days during this fickle season can be sunny and 70° F. or snowy with highs in the 20s. In the low elevations, snows of 1" or more occur 1-5 times a year. At Newfound Gap, 69" fall on average. Lows of -20° are possible in the high country. Major snow storms often leave backpackers stranded at the high elevations, especially in Appalachian Trail shelters.

DAY HIKER'S CHECKLIST

CLOTHING—The one essential piece of equipment for hiking in the Smokies is a rain jacket or poncho. Bring it along even on sunny days when there's not a cloud in the forecast. Sooner or later you'll be thankful you did. During the cooler months, rain pants can also be a big help. In warm weather, however, they tend to lead to overheating.

If hiking in the high country between September and May, always carry warm clothing, including hat and gloves. Many a balmy morning has turned into a frigid, wet afternoon on Mt. Le Conte or the Appalachian Trail.

Cotton is not recommended in cold weather or at high elevations. Carry clothing that will keep you warm when wet such as wool or synthetic "fleece."

FOOT WEAR—Truly water-proof boots can be a big plus in the Smokies. Not only will they keep your feet drier during rainy weather, they also give you a little extra assistance when crossing shallow streams.

WATER—Carry two quarts per person on longer hikes, or carry a good water filter. All water obtained in the backcountry must be treated before drinking! Get a filter that is effective against Giardia since it may be present in any spring or stream.

FOOD—Carry high energy snacks and eat often.

MAP—A variety of park trail maps are available at park visitor centers. Keep one in your pack at all times and know how to use it.

FLASHLIGHT—A good flashlight or headlamp are welcome if you are caught out on the trail after dark.

MATCHES—waterproof are best.

EMERGENCY WHISTLE—to signal rescuers when lost. All children should carry one.

CRAMPONS—Small, clip-on crampons can be very helpful when hiking high elevation trails during cold weather.

PETS

Dogs (on a leash) are only allowed on the Gatlinburg and Oconaluftee River trails, neither of which is described in this book.

EASIER HIKES

ANDREWS BALD

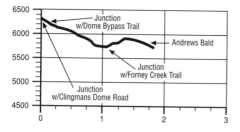

LENGTH: 3.6 miles roundtrip from Clingmans Dome parking area to Andrews Bald and back.

HIGHLIGHTS: Views from bald; azaleas and Catawba rhododendron.

CAUTIONS: Trail is very rocky.

MAP KEY: E 7: USGS quad: Clingmans Dome.

USE: Hiking trail.

TRAILHEAD: Park at the Clingmans Dome parking area at the end of Clingmans Dome Road. The Forney Ridge Trail to Andrews Bald starts near the bulletin board and drinking fountain at the far end of the parking area.

This hike is good for nearly any time in spring, summer, and fall. Try it on a day in May when spring is opening the first wildflowers in this mile-high-plus area. Sometime after the middle of June, flame azalea and Catawba rhododendron bloom on the bald. If you like blueberries, September is the time to go to Andrews. Go in October and look at the gold and purple hills in the far distance.

I recall earlier times when it was a delight to walk through the green gloom of the spruce-fir forest along this trail. It has a different kind of gloom now, the gloom of death of the fir trees, killed by a little creature called the balsam wooly adelgid. It has killed more than 70 percent of the adult firs in the park. At the same time, air pollution has not been kind to the red spruce.

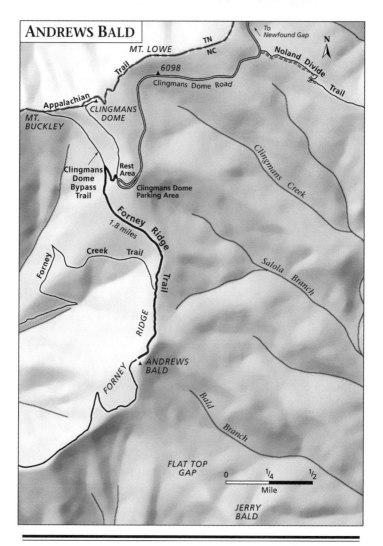

ANDREWS BALD

To Newfound Gap

MT. LOWE

TN
NC

Noland Divide Trail

6098
Clingmans Dome Road

Appalachian Trail

CLINGMANS DOME

MT. BUCKLEY

Clingmans Creek

Clingmans Dome Bypass Trail

Rest Area

Clingmans Dome Parking Area

Forney Ridge

1.8 miles

Forney Creek Trail

Forney

Trail

Salola Branch

FORNEY RIDGE

ANDREWS BALD

Bald Branch

FLAT TOP GAP

0   ¼   ½
Mile

JERRY BALD

N

It is an easy hike. Starting point is the Clingmans Dome parking area. The first part of the trail is the least pleasant. It is steepest and rockiest and it runs through an area of ragged growth that isn't particularly attractive. This is because it was swept by fire in the middle 1920s. However, it's good territory for birders. The Winter Wren, Veery, Dark-eyed Junco and some of the warblers are nearly always present in spring and summer.

Within a half-mile you'll be out of the burned-over area and into the once-lovely spruce-fir forest where the adelgids and pollution have done their dirty work. You will notice that young firs continue to sprout and grow. Many of them live long enough to produce seed from which still more young firs grow.

Notice the little wood-sorrel (*Oxalis montana*) growing thickly in the dark-lace shade in the thick spruce-fir stands. Just before you reach the bald, if you make the trip around the middle of June, you may find tiny wild lilies of the valley.

Like nearly all the grassy balds of the Great Smokies, Andrews has some heath plants. Those you'll be most interested in, if you make the trip during the second half of June—say about June 15-25—are Catawba rhododendron and flame azalea. The rhododendron grows on the higher part of the bald, the part you reach first. To see the best azaleas, walk on down the slope to the southern edge of the bald.

Go in late August or the first half of September for blueberries. They usually ripen over a period of nearly a month. To be certain of the best time to find them in a given season, consult a ranger at the Sugarlands Visitor Center, near Park Headquarters, at Gatlinburg. These are high-bush blueberries. Some of the bushes grow far higher than your head.

Arriving when berries are ripe is no guarantee of finding many berries. Bears may have harvested them. They gorge on them. Just as at Gregory Bald, the forest has been invading Andrews Bald. And just as it is doing at Gregory, the National Park Service is reversing the forest invasion and returning Andrews to a place of mostly grass and scattered azaleas and blueberries.

At about 5,800 feet above sea level, Andrews is the highest grass bald in the park. Most of the other well-known balds in the park— Gregory Bald, Silers Bald and Spence Field—are on the main crest of the Great Smokies, divided between Tennessee and North Carolina. But Andrews is entirely within Carolina.

Of the major grass balds it is the easiest for the hiker to reach. It also offers the best azalea show for small effort in getting there. However, Andrews azaleas don't approach the big display on Gregory.

There are only two intersections on the trail and you take the left fork—on the way to the bald—both times. The first intersection is only a few hundred yards from the parking area. The right fork leads to the Appalachian Trail. The second intersection is near the middle point of the hike. The right fork here goes down to Forney Creek.

View from Andrews Bald.

THE APPALACHIAN TRAIL: NEWFOUND GAP TO ROAD PRONG

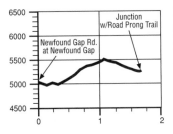

LENGTH: 3.4 miles roundtrip, from Newfound Gap parking area to Road Prong Trail junction and back.

HIGHLIGHTS: Spring wildflowers.

MAP KEY: D 8; USGS Quad: Clingmans Dome.

USE: Hiking trail.

TRAILHEAD: Park at the large Newfound Gap parking area, mid-way between Gatlinburg, TN and Cherokee, NC on the Newfound Gap Road (U.S. 441). After parking, walk across Newfound Gap Road to the Appalachian Trail.

Winter lingers late along the crest of the Great Smokies. Cold winds from the north sometimes carry snow slanting against the north sides of every tree and shrub, leaving that side white and the other side untouched. At other times, the wind carries heavy fog, which freezes and builds up as hoarfrost, a sparkling sight when the sun strikes it the next day.

This hike can be—but not always is—a good winter hike. Try it on a cold, windy day, with maybe a few flakes of snow in the air. Listen to the wind moan, sometimes loud, sometimes low, in the spruce and fir trees that grow along much of the crest.

Park your car at Newfound Gap, and pick up the westward trail a few feet north of the Clingmans Dome Road. This is the Appalachian Trail, which meanders the mountains from Maine to Georgia, including about 70 miles through the highlands of the Great Smokies. A few minutes before you reach Indian Gap, you will come to a wire fence that enclosed a forest of mostly beech trees. Within this beech forest grows one of the park's outstanding displays of spring wildflowers. May usually is the best month to see this display of spring-beau-

APPALACHIAN TRAIL:
NEWFOUND GAP TO ROAD PRONG

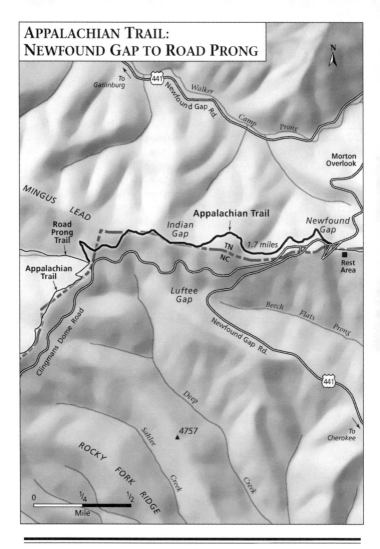

N

To
Gatlinburg

441

Walker

Newfound Gap Rd

Camp

Prong

Morton
Overlook

MINGUS LEAD

Road
Prong
Trail

Indian
Gap

Appalachian Trail

Newfound
Gap

TN
NC

1.7 miles

Appalachian
Trail

Rest
Area

Clingmans Dome Road

Luftee
Gap

Newfound Gap Rd.

Beech Flats Prong

441

To
Cherokee

Deep

▲ 4757

Sahlee
Creek

Creek

ROCKY FORK RIDGE

0   ¼   ½
Mile

ties, trout lilies, blue and yellow violets, and white trillium.

The National Park Service built the fence to keep European wild hogs out of the wildflowers. The hogs are destructive, non-native pests which eat portions of the flowers. They particularly like the corms of the spring-beauties. Their eating and rooting do extensive damage to some of the most beautiful and fragile areas of the park. This, a beech gap, is one of those areas.

The wild hogs are the only animals barred by the fence. Small animals go through it. Larger ones climb over it or jump over it. Short ramps are provided for hikers to cross it.

Spring is another pleasant time to make this hike, though it is good any time—except when it is under several inches of snow. It's a good hot-weather hike because it's never hot up here. Practically all of the trail is more than 5,000 feet above sea level.

One spring-blooming shrub on the trail is hobble bush, spindly and awkward looking as an adolescent boy. It sprouts wrinkly leaves, round and faintly heart-shaped, growing opposite each other. Between the leaves are clusters of white blossoms. In autumn, the leaves are among the first in the forest to change color. They turn every shade from waxy orange-red to dark wine. The bushes have bright red berries in fall.

The junction with Road Prong Trail is the point where an old road once crossed the mountains, linking Tennessee and North Carolina. First an Indian trail, it was widened into a road in the late 1830s and was used until a paved road was built across the mountain at Newfound Gap in the 1920s.

Junction of Appalachian Trail and Road Prong Trail beside Clingmans Dome Road. →

APPALACHIAN TRAIL
Newfound Gap   1.7
Mount Collins Shelter 3.3
Clingmans Dome   6.2

CHEROKEE ORCHARD TO SUGARLANDS

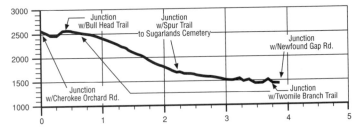

LENGTH: 3.9 miles one way, from Cherokee Orchard Road to Newfound Gap Road (U.S. 441) near Sugarlands Visitor Center. A car shuttle is recommended.

HIGHLIGHTS: Historic sites.

MAP KEY: 6-7 C; USGS quads: Gatlinburg, Mt. Le Conte.

USE: Horse and hiking trail.

TRAILHEAD: From U.S. 441 in downtown Gatlinburg, turn at traffic light #8 onto Historic Nature Trail—Airport Road. After 3.4 miles, just after the road becomes one-way, turn right into the Rainbow Falls & Bullhead trails parking area. Hike Bullhead Trail 0.4 mile to Old Sugarlands Trail.

This hike is pretty easy, unless you plan to make a roundtrip of it, because it's nearly all gradual downhill walking.

You'll be walking much of the way over two old roads that were used by people who lived along them. These are the old Bullhead Road and the Sugarlands Road. The name the route carries now is the Old Sugarlands Trail. Start west from Cherokee Orchard as if you were going to Mt. Le Conte by way of the Bullhead Trail, but instead of turning south on the Bullhead Trail, continue west on what is now the Old Sugarlands Trail.

If you happen to do the hike in July, you may see mountain pepper-bush and rosebay rhododendron blooming near the Bullhead Trail intersection.

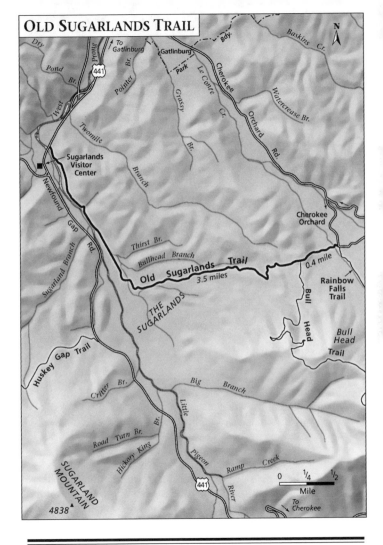

OLD SUGARLANDS TRAIL

N

Dry Pond Br.

West Prong

441

To Gatlinburg

Pointer Br.

Gatlinburg

Park Bdy.

Baskins Cr.

Le Conte Cr.

Grassy Br.

Cherokee Orchard Rd.

Watercrease Br.

Twomile Branch

Sugarlands Visitor Center

Newfound Gap Rd.

Sugarland Branch Rd.

Thirst Br.

Bullhead Branch

Old Sugarlands Trail

3.5 miles

0.4 mile

Cherokee Orchard

Rainbow Falls Trail

THE SUGARLANDS

Bull Head

Bull Head Trail

Huskey Gap Trail

Critter Br.

Road Turn Br.

Hickory King Br.

Big Branch

Little Pigeon River

Ramp Creek

441

To Cherokee

SUGARLAND MOUNTAIN

4838

0   1/4   1/2
Mile

The Sugarlands Cemetery sits atop a small hill.

A few minutes later, you'll see first one and then another trail leading to the right. Ignore them. Horses use them a great deal and chop up portions of them badly.

Your walk is through a second-growth forest that includes maples, hemlocks, oaks, hickories, tuliptrees, dogwoods, blackgums, sourwoods and other tree species. At mile **2.2**, notice rock walls, an abandoned garbage dump, and the ruins of foundations and bridges. This area is the site of two Sugarlands CCC Camps (NP-2 and NP-10) that operated here from June 1, 1933 to July 18, 1942. According to records in the park archives, the Sugarlands CCC crews had a strong sense of community and even published a newsletter of jokes and songs. The company built the stone arch bridge over the West Prong of the Little Pigeon River, which you will cross at the end of the hike. A sketch of the bridge was presented to President Franklin Roosevelt.

Farther along, you come to a broad, level side trail that leads to the stately Sugarlands Cemetery and to the site of the Pi Beta Phi Settlement School, built out of the old Brackins Log School. During the turn of the century, the Pi Beta Phi Sorority, founded at William and Mary College, extended aid to the people near Gatlinburg. According to one brochure, these college women (or do-gooders, as they were called in the mountains) were devoted to "scientific, humanized service."

By mile **2.6** you'll be within sound and sight of the West Prong of Little Pigeon River, the stream that parallels the lower section of the Tennessee portion of the highway to Newfound Gap. And by then, you will be on an older transmountain highway, the Old Sugarland Road. The state of Tennessee built this highway in the late 1920s. The National Park Service decided in the 1930s that the highway did not meet its standards and replaced it with the present highway. The portions of the old road you walk are on the opposite side of the stream from the present highway.

Within an hour and a half to two hours of starting (or less time if you hurry), you should arrive at the newer highway, just down the road from Sugarlands Visitor Center.

DEEP CREEK - INDIAN CREEK LOOP

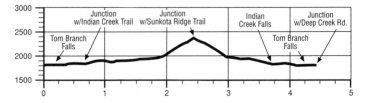

LENGTH: 4.4-mile-long loop hike.
HIGHLIGHTS: Waterfalls, wildflowers.
CAUTIONS: Don't climb on waterfalls.
MAP KEY: 7F, USGS QUADS: Bryson City, Clingmans Dome
USE: Horse and hiking trail.
TRAILHEAD: From downtown Bryson City, NC, follow the signs to Deep Creek Campground. Continue past the campground entrance (don't take the bridge across the creek) to the hiker parking area at the end of the road. Deep Creek Trail is the old road that starts at the far end of the hiker parking area.

This might be called the "Hearts-A-Bustin'-With-Love Hike" or the "Waterfall Hike."

If you do it in late summer or early autumn, you'll find hearts-a-bustin'-with-love (*Euonymus americanus*) displaying rose-pink shells and orange-red berries every few yards along the entire hike. This little wild shrub grows very well in this area. The National Park Service has planted several clumps of it in Deep Creek Campground.

The campground is about three miles north of Bryson City, NC. Deep Creek Trail starts a few yards north of the campground and runs to the left of and parallel to Deep Creek. You'll see your first waterfall about 1,000 feet beyond the trail start.

This is Toms Branch Falls. Lovely! An expert landscaper couldn't have done half as well as nature did. The small stream tumbles 60 or 70 feet into Deep Creek on the side of the creek opposite the trail. The fall is broken into a half-dozen rock-ledge levels. When

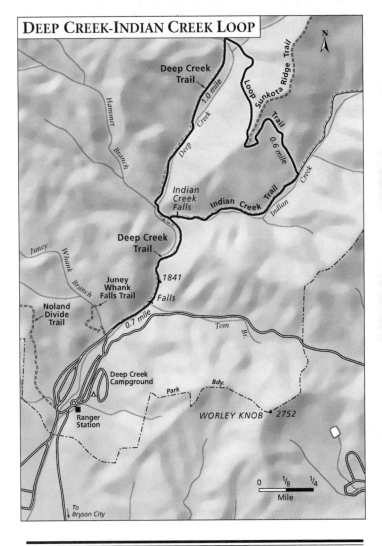

DEEP CREEK-INDIAN CREEK LOOP

N

Deep Creek
Trail

1.0 mile

Loop
Trail

Sunkota Ridge Trail

0.6 mile

Hammer

Branch

Deep Creek

Indian
Creek
Falls

Indian Creek Trail

Indian Creek

Deep Creek
Trail

Juney

Whank Branch

Juney
Whank
Falls Trail

1841

Falls

Noland
Divide
Trail

0.7 mile

Tom Br.

Deep Creek
Campground

Park Bdy.

WORLEY KNOB 2752

Ranger
Station

0   1/8   1/4
Mile

To
Bryson City

Indian Creek Falls.

the stream is low, the water switches from one side to the other between drops.

Your trail once was an old motor road for the first mile and a half. It switches back and forth across the creek a few times by way of wooden bridges.

Follow it three-quarters mile, to the point where the trail forks, the right fork going up Indian Creek and the left one up Deep Creek. Although you could simply go a short distance up Indian Creek to Indian Creek Falls, I suggest you go left and make a loop of it. Notice the sand and rocks on the trail. Those slivery particles are mica.

In springtime you'll see trillium, Solomon's seal, false Solomon's seal, dog hobble, violets, Jack-in-the-pulpit, dogwoods and other spring flowers in bloom along this trail. Some grow to giant size. I saw a Solomon's seal six feet tall when pulled straight up from its normal bent posture. Dogwoods are particularly numerous along the Deep Creek leg of the loop.

Fall flowers here include many asters, golden rod, iron weed, blue lobelia and cardinal flower.

Watch for the marker for Loop Trail onto which you turn right. It's only a dozen feet beyond a bridge over which you cross to the right of the creek.

Follow Loop Trail 1.2 miles over Sunkota Ridge to Indian Creek Trail. Loop Trail has enough laurel and rhododendron for a fine show in years when bloom is good. Also, look along it for trailing arbutus and galax.

This is second-growth timber, with pines and oaks predominating, along the ridge trail. Near the intersection of Loop Trail and Indian Creek Trail is the stone foundation of a building, but the building is gone. This area once was inhabited. Indian Creek School stood somewhere in this vicinity, according to old maps.

Turn right on the trail and follow it down Indian Creek to the falls, a pretty cascade which ends in a wide pool. A little farther, at the intersection with Deep Creek Trail, you turn left to return to the Deep Creek trailhead.

KEPHART PRONG TRAIL

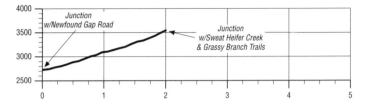

LENGTH: 4.0 miles roundtrip, from Newfound Gap Road to Kephart Prong Shelter and back.

HIGHLIGHTS: Remains of a Civilian Conservation Corps Camp, fish hatchery, and narrow gauge railroad.

MAP KEY: 8 D; USGS quad: Smokemont.

USE: Horse and hiking trail.

TRAILHEAD: Drive on Newfound Gap Road about 8.8 miles south from Newfound Gap or 5.0 miles north from Smokemont Campground. The parking area, a small crescent on the east side, will be on the left from Newfound Gap or the right from Smokemont. The trail starts at the large footbridge over the Oconaluftee River.

A riverine stroll. The translation of the Cherokee word "Oconaluftee"—by the river— accurately describes this trail along a branch of the Oconaluftee River. The trail follows Kephart Prong from its confluence with the Oconaluftee up toward the Appalachian Trail. It provides access (via Grassy Branch and Dry Sluice Gap trails), particularly for day hikers wanting to avoid Newfound Gap crowds, to Charlies Bunion, an outcrop offering panoramic views of both the Tennessee and North Carolina sides of the park. Kephart Prong Trail gains only 830' elevation, and your ascent is so gradual that you rarely sense a climb.

The prong, trail, and mountain above them are named to honor Horace Kephart, author of *Our Southern Highlanders*, a classic portrait of mountain culture during the first decade of the twentieth century. An author, scholar, and librarian from St. Louis, Kephart came to the

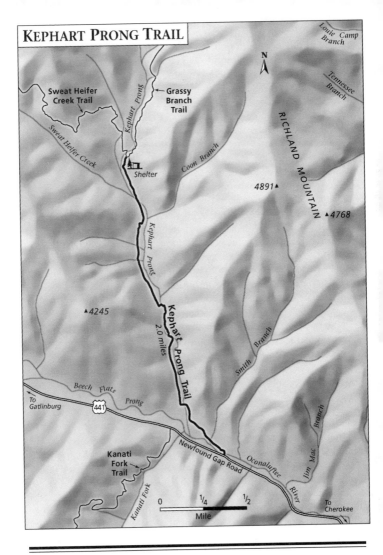

KEPHART PRONG TRAIL

Louie Camp
Branch

Tennessee
Branch

Sweat Heifer
Creek Trail

Grassy
Branch
Trail

Kephart Prong

Sweat Heifer Creek

Coon Branch

RICHLAND MOUNTAIN

Shelter

4891▲

▲4768

Kephart Prong

▲4245

Kephart Prong Trail
2.0 miles

Smith Branch

Beech Flats Prong

To
Gatlinburg

441

Kanati Fork
Trail

Newfound Gap Road

Oconaluftee River

Jim Mac Branch

Kanati Fork

To
Cherokee

N

0   ¼   ½
Mile

Smokies in 1904 after a nervous collapse, which seems mostly to have been a mid-life crisis and shift in values. Leaving his wife and family, he lived alone in the mountains and wrote lovingly and honestly about the Appalachian settlers and land. He was also a leading park advocate in the 1920s.

Kephart Prong Trail crosses Oconaluftee River immediately on a wide bridge surrounded by rosebay rhododendron and Eastern hemlock. The trail is wide, flat, and surfaced with gravel. It was once a paved jeep road; that's why you'll see patches of broken asphalt throughout. Maidenhair and Christmas ferns, daisy fleabane and black-eyed Susan decorate the gentle slope.

None of the trees here are very big because this trail was logged and later became the location of a Civilian Conservation Corps Camp from 1933-1942. During World War II, the camp housed conscientious objectors. The compound included barracks, officers' quarters, latrine, mess hall, educational and recreational buildings, and a woodworking shop. You'll see evidence of the camp at **0.2** mile where large boxwoods mark a front yard on the right. Behind them stands a 6' x 5' sign plaque made of stream-rounded and now moss-covered stones under an oak tree. A stone water fountain, well-preserved except that it doesn't work, is a few steps ahead, just before another, much larger hearth and chimney in the center of an Eastern hemlock stand. Constructed of brick and stone with a cook surface in front, this one is about 15' wide.

After the camp, the trail narrows to about a yard's width. In short succession, two offshoot trails lead you to the creek, the second to a small pebble "beach." The trail itself is surrounded by tuliptrees and oaks, with lots of may-apples underneath. Mountain folklore says that an unmarried girl who pulls up this attractive wildflower will become pregnant. Blooming may-apple plants have two prominent leaves under which a small white flower blooms in early spring and from which the "apple" grows afterwards. Non-blooming plants have only one leaf. Both grow anywhere from 18"-30" tall.

Soon you reach a fork in the trail. Take the left one; a burned oak trunk blocks the right option to a spur trail that peters out on a hillside. In a couple of minutes, you'll round a curve to the first prong

A remnant of the Civilian Conservation Corps camp.

crossing; you can wade across or take the railed footbridge a bit further up. The bridge itself is sturdy although you might test the rail before you depend on it. It wobbles. You'll walk through a second-growth tuliptree forest with lots of wood betony, a spring wildflower whose leaves look very much like a fern's, growing below. Other common names for this plant are lousewort and, logically, fernleaf. Look up to the left to see a grass-covered roadbed.

At **0.7** mile, you'll see a cement platform with a two-foot square well in one corner up a steep bank on the left. To the right, you'll spy another cement platform. These platforms may be the remains of a cistern to a fish hatchery run by the Works Progress Administration in the 1930s. The hatchery supplied trout and bass to overfished park streams. A successful project, in December 1936, 50,000 trout eggs were hatched here. An archive photograph shows dozens of round, stone-encircled rearing pools spaced along the slope of a grassy streambank, but no vestige of these pools remains in the rebounding forest.

At **1.0** mile the trail becomes a corridor of tall, slender American beech trees with ferns below on the stream bank. The trail moves at a slow incline, its surface pebbles and rocks. When the bank becomes steep, the corridor veers in and out of Eastern hemlock groves and heath slicks. A nice view of Kephart Prong appears on the right with cascade falls. Within the next half mile come four stream crossings; wade across or continue 30 paces up the trail to the foot bridges, some buttressed by CCC stonework.

During the final 0.2 mile, you'll notice lichen-covered railroad irons scattered alongside. They are the remains of a narrow gauge railroad that Champion Fibre Company built up the prong for removing spruce lumber from the 2,200 acres it clear-cut in the 1920s. Now delicate rue-anemone lines the trail. In July crimson bee-balm and its white cousin, wild bergamot, add bright blooms to the understory. At one point a rivulet runs alongside, then through, the trail and ultimately finds the prong. It's a good place to see dusky salamanders.

As the trail rises a bit, it becomes eroded and dominated by roots, rocks, and mud. Then it dries, the pebbles change to flint, and the shelter, once the location of a logging camp, comes into view under American beech trees. It has two sleeping platforms and an indoor fireplace.

A signed trail junction connects to Grassy Branch Trail. Sweat Heifer Creek Trail can be found around the left end of the shelter and across a foot log.

ROAD PRONG TRAIL

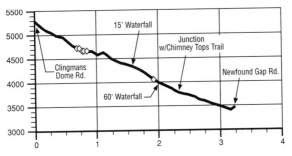

LENGTH: 3.3 miles one way, from Clingmans Dome Road to the Chimney Tops trailhead. A car shuttle is recommended.
HIGHLIGHTS: Waterfalls, big trees, spruce-fir forest.
CAUTIONS: Rocky trail, one moderately difficult creek crossing.
MAP KEY: 7 D; USGS quads: Mt. Le Conte, Clingmans Dome.
USE: Hiking trail.
STARTING POINT: Park at the history exhibit parking area on Clingmans Dome Road, 1.7 miles from Newfound Gap Road. Look for the large parking area and interpretive sign on the right.

Let's suppose you want to break away for two or three hours from the cares of complex civilization. You want to walk through a green curtain into a land of 10,000 years ago, a wilderness of trees, flowers, mosses, ferns, brooks, birds, and solitude.

Put on some boots that can take getting wet. Take along a sandwich. You're going down the Road Prong Trail, sometimes called the Old Indian Road, from Clingmans Dome Road to the Chimney Tops trailhead (on Newfound Gap Road).

Unless you don't mind retracing your steps, work out an arrangement whereby you can leave your car at the Chimney Tops parking area, where you'll end the hike, and ride with someone else to the starting point. To reach the starting point, leave the Newfound Gap Road at Newfound Gap and drive westward about two miles on the

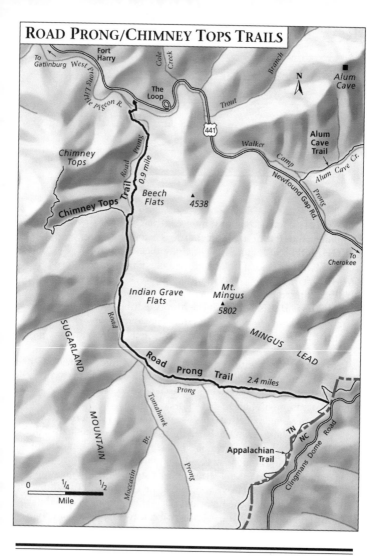

ROAD PRONG/CHIMNEY TOPS TRAILS

To Gatlinburg

Fort Harry

West Prong Little Pigeon R.

Cole Creek

The Loop

441

Trout

N

Alum Cave

Walker

Camp

Alum Cave Trail

Chimney Tops

Road Prong Trail

0.9 mile

Beech Flats

▲ 4538

Chimney Tops

Newfound Gap Rd.

Alum Cave Cr.

To Cherokee

Indian Grave Flats

Mt. Mingus
▲ 5802

SUGARLAND

Road

Road Prong Trail   2.4 miles

MINGUS LEAD

MOUNTAIN

Prong

Tomahawk

Br.

Prong

TN
NC

Appalachian Trail

Clingmans Dome Road

Maccasin

0   ¼   ½
Mile

Clingmans Dome Road.

It was at this gap that the first road crossed the high Smokies. And before there was a road, there was a trail, an Indian trail which Cherokees and perhaps other Indians walked farther back in time than anyone will ever know.

White settlers widened the trail into a road in 1839 and it became a toll road over which horse-drawn vehicles rolled and droves of cattle, hogs and other livestock passed en route to market.

According to some sources, Confederate Cherokee troops under the command of Col. William H. Thomas improved the road during the Civil War. Thomas, a white man adopted by the Cherokees when he was a youth, became chief of the Cherokees in North Carolina. This road was used until the late 1920s, when a new road was built across the mountain at Newfound Gap.

However, time and many freezes and thaws have left only a trail where the old road existed. Faint though the trail is at some places, you can't get lost. For the trail is always within sight or sound of a tumbling stream, which goes on to join a larger stream at a point only a few yards from where your car is parked.

The trail starts at the 5,272-foot level, eight feet less than a mile high. One stream follows it down the north (Tennessee) side of the mountains to the connection with the Newfound Gap Road at about the 3,600-foot level. The stream begins a few yards down the mountain from the trail beginning. Trail and creek cross several times without benefit of foot bridges.

The stream is Road Prong of the West Prong of Little Pigeon River. Fed by numerous springs, it quickly grows larger and noisier. It jumps over falls and throws itself in foamy frolic at moss-topped boulders. It soon grows large enough to support brook trout, lovely little fish with orange bellies and cherry-red dots along their sides. They are natives and so were their ancestors. They were here thousands of years before the first fish ever saw the inside of a hatchery truck. Because their numbers have dwindled at an alarming rate in recent years, it now is illegal to fish for them in most streams in this national park.

Along the trail is primeval forest. All around are the sights, sounds and fragrances of nature. Man's only visible mark here is the dim trail that once was a road.

A Rose-breasted Grosbeak, his chest colored with crimson as if his throat were cut, sits on a branch of a big yellow birch and sings the same song his ancestors sang in another birch at about the same spot thousands of years before Columbus learned to read the stars.

At one point, the trail snakes high along a hillside, overlooking the creek. Curving down the opposite hillside is something of such graceful design one might think it the work of an expert landscaper. It's a tiny stream, swiftly plunging down a curving stair-stepped bed of rock, foaming white its entire length.

A little more than a mile from the beginning of the trail is Indian Grave Flats, where one of Col. Thomas's men was buried.

At **1.6** miles there is evidence of a massive landslide and log jam caused by an isolated cloudburst in the 1990s.

A little farther downstream, you will come to an area where civilization once reached. Farmers tilled the rocky valley before it was purchased for the park. If you search, you may find a sweet-smelling purple-fringed orchid blooming along here in June or early July.

Near the end of your hike, this trail intersects the trail to the chimneys. Continue downstream (right).

A short time later, you'll be back to people, pavement and exhaust fumes. So don't hurry.

MODERATE HIKES

ABRAMS FALLS

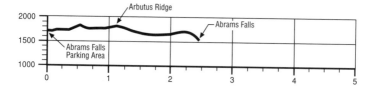

LENGTH: 5.0 miles roundtrip, from the trailhead in Cades Cove to Abrams Falls and back.
HIGHLIGHTS: Abrams Creek and Abrams Falls.
CAUTIONS: Do not climb on slippery rocks around falls.
MAP KEY: 2 D; USGS quads: Cades Cove, Calderwood.
USE: Hiking trail.
TRAILHEAD: Turn right onto unpaved side road between sign posts #10 and #11 on the one-way Cades Cove Loop Road. The side road terminates in large trailhead parking area. Be forewarned, during the busy season, traffic on the loop road may make travel annoyingly slow.

Abrams Creek plunges over Abrams Falls into one of the largest natural pools in the park. Flecked white dancing bubbles of foam, deep and cold and bordered with ledges of gray rock, it is a lovely place to see.

Abrams Creek is the largest stream entirely inside the park. It drains an area considered by many to be the most beautiful in the park—Cades Cove and the mountains around it.

Abrams Creek, which borders the trail, and Abrams Falls were named for Cherokee Chief Abram. He lived in the village of Chilhowee at the mouth of Abrams Creek on the Little Tennessee River. This place is now beneath the waters of Chilhowee Lake.

The stream has dozens of tributaries and their names range the alphabet from Anthony Creek to Wildcat Branch. Many tumble clear and cold and boisterous down the mountainside into the cove. There they slow their pace, join the main stream and meander quietly

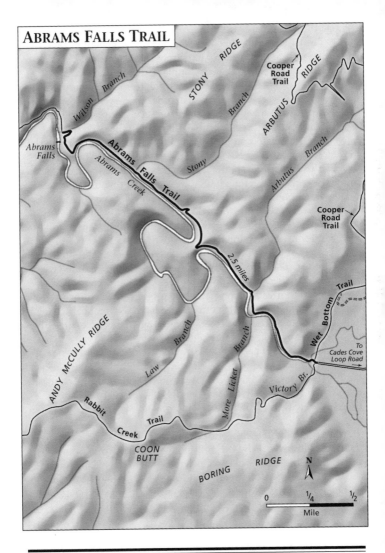

ABRAMS FALLS TRAIL

Wilson Branch

STONY RIDGE

Cooper Road Trail

ARBUTUS RIDGE

Abrams Falls

Abrams Falls Trail

Abrams Creek

Stony Branch

Arbutus Branch

Cooper Road Trail

2.5 miles

Wet Bottom Trail

To Cades Cove Loop Road

ANDY McCULLY RIDGE

Law Branch

More Licker Branch

Victory Br.

Rabbit Creek Trail

COON BUTT

BORING RIDGE

N

0   1/4   1/2
Mile

through the flat-to-gently rolling cove. Deer drink from the creek.

On its trip through the cove, Abrams Creek encounters lime-stone, uncommon in the park. Many trout fishermen think Abrams Creek, below the cove, is the best fishing stream in the park. Some ichthyologists say the limestone factor is the reason trout grow a little larger there, on average, than those in other park streams. They say limestone provides a better habitat for the small creatures trout eat.

Brook trout are the only native salmonid in the park. John Oliver, the great-grandson of the John Oliver who was an early settler in Cades Cove, stocked 10,000 rainbow trout fingerlings in Abrams Creek in 1908. These were the first rainbow planted in waters now inside the park. At the time John Oliver released the rainbows, it was believed that non-native rainbow trout and brook trout could success-fully coexist, but the larger rainbows bullied the native brookies into retreating upstream. Brookies now live in the small streams in the high elevations, while rainbows dominate lower streams.

Since the early 1900s, brook trout have lost about 75% of their range in the park due to logging and the introduction of rainbow trout. The park has restored brook trout populations to a number of lower elevation streams. Non-native trout species are first removed from the stream, then brookies are reintroduced. Natural barriers such as waterfalls prevent re-invasion of non-native trout species once the brookies have become reestablished

Hikers who also happen to be trout fishermen may want to take part of this hike in the creek. But a word of warning: Abrams Creek has the slipperiest bottom of any stream in the mountains. And a fish-erman must stay in the creek most of the way, for the banks are so thickly covered with laurel, rhododendron and trees that casting from them is very difficult.

Much of the trail is easy, with a fairly even grade down close to the creek. However, at two or three points, the trail crosses piny ridges, while the creek makes wide detours round them. The second rise is over Arbutus Ridge, named for trailing arbutus—one of the ear-liest blooming spring flowers. The trail crosses a dip in the crest of

Abrams Falls →

Arbutus Ridge at mile **0.8**. Here you'll be hearing the creek far down to your left rear. Then, after taking another step or two, as the trail twists to the right, you'll hear the creek roar from a different direction, your left front. A look at the map will show you that the creek traveled more than a mile, in a wide loop, from where you heard it two steps back to where you hear it now.

Descending from Arbutus Ridge, watch for a display of unusual wildflowers in spring. Huge clusters of bleeding heart rise up against the rocky cliffs. But even more delightful are the tiny pink blossoms of gay-wings.

Abrams Falls is a delight to see, especially in high water. By the time Abrams Creek tumbles over Abrams Falls, it is carrying lots of water. It drops approximately 20 feet from the lip of the ledge to a dark, broad pool more than a hundred feet across.

This is a good hike for any season, but it is especially good in late May. Hiker-fishermen then find Abrams Creek waters warmed enough to be pleasant. And this is the time mountain laurel usually blooms along the creek and trail.

An odd thing about the laurel bloom is a method by which its pollen is scattered. You can help do the scattering. Notice the stamens, the small filaments coming up from the center of the flower. You'll see that the stamen ends, called the anthers, fit into tiny notches in the corolla, the inner portion of the single fused petal. Take a twig or pencil tip and dislodge an anther from its notch, and see the tiny shower of pollen. Insects normally do the task you did with the pencil.

Another good flower that blooms about the same time is sweet shrub, a small bush which has maroon flowers. They are so fragrant that the ladies of Cades Cove once used the petals as perfume.

ALBRIGHT GROVE LOOP

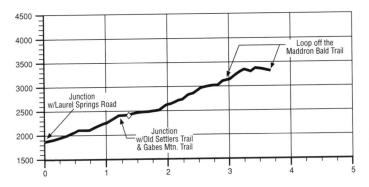

LENGTH: 6.8 miles roundtrip from Maddron Bald trailhead to Albright Grove loop, around the loop, and back.

HIGHLIGHTS: Virgin forest.

MAP KEY: 9 D; USGS quad: Mt. Guyot.

USE: Hiking trail.

TRAILHEAD: Drive U.S. 321 15.5 miles east from Gatlinburg or 2.8 miles west from Cosby to Baxter Road, which is 0.1 mile east of Yogi's Campground. Keep to the right until you reach the marked park trailhead. There is only room for four or five cars, and they may not be safe; several vehicles have been stolen from here and recycled at a local chop shop. Safe parking (for a fee) may be available at businesses on U.S. 321. Do not park on private property without permission. Hike Maddron Bald Trail for 2.9 miles to Albright Grove Loop Trail.

The first 2.3 miles of Maddron Bald Trail are along an old road and offer pleasant, easy walking with Buckeye Creek on your left. At first the right side of the trail is dark with young Eastern hemlocks so thick that there are no ground plants, but soon the forest opens up with small American beeches, maples, and tuliptrees. This area was heavily

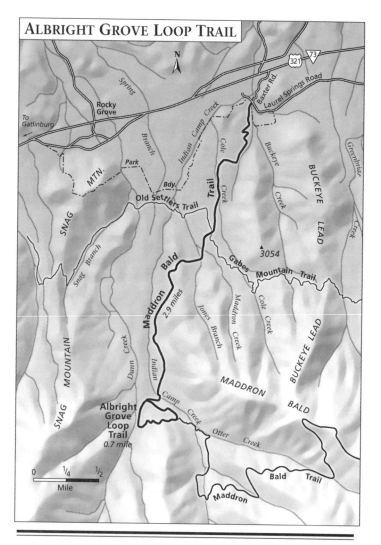

ALBRIGHT GROVE LOOP TRAIL

N

To Gatlinburg

Spring Branch

Rocky Grove

321 73

Baxter Rd.

Laurel Springs Road

Indian Camp Creek

Cole Creek

Buckeye Creek

Greenbriar Creek

BUCKEYE LEAD

SNAG MTN.

Park

Bdy.

Old Settlers Trail

Trail

Branch

3054

Gabes Mountain Trail

SNAG MOUNTAIN

Snag Branch

Maddron Bald

2.9 miles

Jones Branch

Maddron Creek

Cole Creek

BUCKEYE LEAD

Dunn Creek

Indian

Camp Creek

MADDRON BALD

Albright Grove Loop Trail
0.7 mile

Otter Creek

Bald Trail

Maddron

0   1/4   1/2

Mile

farmed and had large corn fields and apple orchards. In 1929, the Tennessee Park Commission paid landowner Marshall Justus $4,750 for 109 acres near Albright Grove. Justus had a barn, a five-room frame house, an apple house, 685 apple trees, a tenant house, two corn cribs, and a woodshed. This was one of the 6,600 separate land purchases necessary to establish the national park.

A Civilian Conservation Corps crew lived at the base of this trail from 1933-35 and built most of the trails and bridges in this area. Their culverts, waterbars, and trail engineering efforts make this trail a delight to hike; the trail to Albright Grove is dry and well-graded.

The trail rises above the creek and at about 0.7 mile, it levels as it passes the Willis Baxter cabin on the right. This one room cabin, built in 1889, has a shake roof, two doors, and a healthy population of mud wasps. At the turn-of-the-century, Alex and Sara Baxter and their four sons lived in this cabin. They raised pigs, apples, corn, and sweet potatoes. All the original wood for this cabin was American chestnut, possibly all from one tree. American chestnuts with circumferences of 33' were recorded in this area before the blight.

The present cabin has been restored with some pine and tuliptree, but the walls, ceiling joists, and rafters are the original chestnut. Most cabins built at this time had at least one window, at the very least a small granny window beside the fireplace. From this window, the granny of the house could keep in touch with family members outside without leaving the warmth of the fire. But the Baxter cabin doesn't even have that and must have been pretty dark on cold winter days. However, as Horace Kephart wrote in *Our Southern Highlanders*, "no mountain cabin needs a window to ventilate it: there are cracks and catholes everywhere, …the doors are always open except at night."

Plants that probably came up this valley with the settlers are still here in front of the cabin: clover, heal-all, plantain, dandelion, and poison ivy. The poison ivy is native, but it couldn't venture into woodlands without the help of farming disturbances. Beyond the cabin is a large field of second growth tuliptrees mixed with a few maples and locusts. Arthur Stupka, park naturalist from 1935 to 1964, states that this kind of forest, with 80% tuliptree, usually marks the site of a former corn and potato field.

The trail crosses Cole Creek, which supplied the cabin with water, and then rises, entering Eastern hemlock and rosebay rhododendron forest again. Look for patches of Indian pipe, or ghostflower, in this area. This non-photosynthetic plant flowers in July, and the grayish stalks may be visible until October.

The trail rises again and levels at a wider place at mile **1.2**. Here Gabes Mountain Trail goes left and Old Settlers Trail goes right. Maddron Bald Trail continues straight through a row of three boulders that looks more like a roadblock than a natural geological formation. It becomes narrower and mossier and crosses several small creeks, but the CCC culverts will keep your feet dry. Open woods near these creeks encourage wildflower growth. Then the trail continues on a long level stretch with dense Eastern hemlock and rosebay rhododendron on the left and open deciduous woods on the right. After a sharp right switchback, you climb away from Maddron Creek drainage and toward Indian Camp Creek drainage.

The trail seems to fork, but it is just an old traffic turnaround. Either fork leads to the next Maddron Bald Trail sign. Before you step off the old road bed onto the forest trail, look around at the skinny trees, mostly tuliptrees with a few maples and small hemlocks. This is the end of the settlement road and the end of the cut-over look.

Now proceed on a real trail, rising gently from the end of the road. There are a few roots and rocks, but it is still easy walking. Bigger trees, mostly Eastern hemlock at the beginning, appear, and the deeper woods muffle the creek sounds and your footsteps. A tree fall and a creek crossing have made a wild garden with foamflower, blue cohosh, violets, hepatica, Fraser's sedge, and clubmosses. Farther along there are American beech trees and beech drops (brownish many-branched six-to-ten-inch-tall flowering plants that are parasitic on beech roots), a big patch of Fraser's sedge, and several decaying nurse logs. When competition for land and light is fierce, saplings on nurse logs get a boost. And later, when the nurse log rots, successful saplings look as if they are standing up on their roots.

The trail climbs a small ridge and finally you can see Indian Camp Creek through the rosebay rhododendron. Descend to the creek with a view of a large creek island and then cross the creek on a good, bouncy foot log. After passing another big patch of Fraser's sedge, the trail rises sharply and then levels at the junction of Maddron Bald and Albright Grove Loop trails.

Turn right on the loop, which was named for Horace Albright, the second director of the National Park Service. Albright, a lawyer and conservationist, was an early advocate of a park in the Smokies, believing that national parks should be distributed around the country to serve more people. He helped mediate land condemnation conflicts, participated in the development of the park, and defied the efforts of Senator McKellar of Tennessee to design a state line crest highway for the Smokies. He was also a good friend of John D. Rockefeller, Jr. and gave him professional advice during 35 years of conservation philanthropy, including enabling gifts to the Smokies, Acadia, Shenandoah, Grand Teton, and at least 20 other parks. Albright deserves to have this beautiful grove named for him.

The narrow Albright Grove Loop Trail twists and rises along a small creek. The Eastern hemlock canopy overhead and the needle carpet provide an atmosphere even in winter that seems to require whispering. Tuliptrees, Fraser magnolias, and maples have grown into giants here, in a virgin forest that Champion Fibre Company once owned, but sold to the park commission after a condemnation suit.

Look at how different trees have made adaptations to support massive trunks. Beech trees send out buttress roots; silverbell trees bulge at the base; and Fraser magnolias extend roots that look like big toes. As the trail levels and starts down, look for a giant tuliptree on the left (mile **3.2**) with a little spur trail made by admirers. A few yards farther down the trail stands the real giant of this trail, a tuliptree with a circumference of more than 25', or five to seven people stretching and grasping hands. However, this tree would no longer interest Champion Fibre. Its crown has been broken off, probably by lightning, and it lives with just a few lower branches. An elderberry shrub is thriving 50' up on the broken trunk, and from the downhill side, you can see ferns and mosses growing up there. You don't have to go to the tropics to see epiphytes (plants growing high up on other plants) or buttress roots.

The main trail continues past more big silverbells and Eastern hemlocks. In April, silverbell flowers carpet the trail. In fall, look for the light brown fruits about the size of an almond. Each fruit has four wings; it looks like it might be useful for the back end of a dart.

The trail comes up to a ridge where a sign indicates a right turn. Look for a big Fraser magnolia to the left of the sign. It has a mass of stump roots, and some of them look as if they are impatient for the old tree to fall over. After passing a few more giant Eastern hemlocks and silverbells, the trail makes a rough, rocky descent to the Maddron Bald Trail and a trail sign.

← *A giant tuliptree in Albright Grove.*

Boogerman Loop

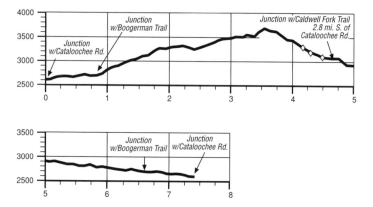

LENGTH: 7.4 mile-long loop hike.

HIGHLIGHTS: Old-growth forests, stone walls, views of Cataloochee Divide.

CAUTIONS: Deep mud, stream crossings.

MAP KEY: 11 D and 11E; USGS quads: Dellwood, Cove Creek Gap.

USE: Horse and hiking trail.

CATALOOCHEE ROAD TRAILHEAD: From I-40, take exit 20 (NC-276) west to Cove Creek Road. Follow Cove Creek north and then west about 7.0 miles toward the Cataloochee Ranger Station. The trailhead lies to the left between Cataloochee Campground and the ranger station.

Your hike begins on the Caldwell Fork Trail and almost immediately crosses Cataloochee Creek on a long foot bridge over 25' in length—reputedly the park's longest log bridge. This trail is noteworthy for its many stream crossings (most via foot bridges). Good boots and careful foot placement will keep you dry on most days. Since Caldwell Fork Trail is both a hiking and horse trail, you should also be prepared for deep mud in places.

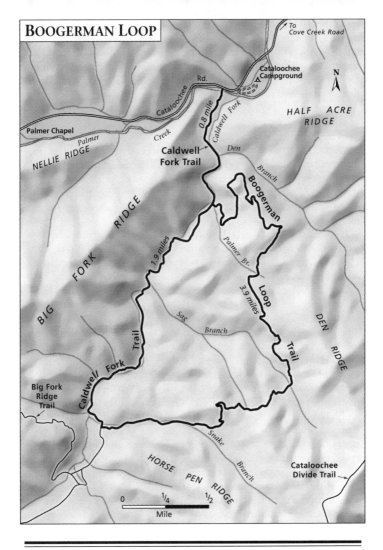

BOOGERMAN LOOP

To
Cove Creek Road

Cataloochee
Campground

N

HALF ACRE
RIDGE

Cataloochee Rd.

Caldwell Fork

0.8 mile

Palmer Chapel

Palmer   Creek

Den

Branch

NELLIE RIDGE

Caldwell
Fork Trail

Boogerman

BIG FORK RIDGE

1.9 miles

Palmer Br.

Loop

3.9 miles

Trail

DEN   RIDGE

Sag   Branch

Caldwell Fork   Trail

Big Fork
Ridge
Trail

Snake   Branch

HORSE PEN RIDGE

Cataloochee
Divide Trail

0   ¼   ½
Mile

Caldwell Fork is named for the second group of permanent settlers to reach the Cataloochee area. In 1841, Levi B. Colwell and his father James Colwell arrived in this valley from Madison County, NC. Eventually, the family began spelling their name "Caldwell," but it is still generally pronounced "Ca'well." Eldridge Caldwell, a grandson, described the primitive condition of his forebears' lives: "When they came in there, they just brought their rifle and their ax and their pot to cook in. So they practically lived on wild meat and fish."

The trail generally follows the Caldwell Fork creek, leading through a cool and shady grove of white pines, then through a brighter hardwood forest before entering a clearing. It continues into another forest of white pines. Many have died and fallen, providing shelter and food for abundant wildlife. Poison ivy, Virginia creeper, ebony spleenwort, Christmas fern, and striped pipsissewa grow in the pines' shade.

At **0.8** miles you reach the junction of Boogerman Trail. Turn left. The trail was named after Robert "Booger" Palmer, who lived nearby. He was just a schoolchild when a teacher in Big Cataloochee School asked him what he wanted to be when he grew up. "I want to be the Boogerman," he said. "Don't you want to be something else besides the Boogerman?" asked the teacher. "No," he says, "That's what I want to be." The nickname stuck.

Because "Booger" Palmer, the former owner of much of this property, did not allow it to be logged, many huge trees grace Boogerman Trail. The trail is exclusively for hikers, and thus is free of the serious erosion found along Caldwell Fork Trail.

Boogerman Trail starts by crossing two small rivulets among dog-hobble and rosebay rhododendron. You climb slightly uphill through an Eastern hemlock forest, its understory featuring witch-hazel and striped maple; on the trail's banks are galax, wood-sorrel, striped pipsissewa, and Christmas fern. Further up you encounter tuliptrees, several species of oaks, and yellow birches. Look for ghost-like Indian pipe rising among dead leaves. This plant, lacking chlorophyll, feeds on rotting vegetation. At a break in the trees, Cataloochee Divide appears in the distance. Soon tall white pines tower overhead and fallen needles perfume the air.

At approximately **1.3** miles, the trail winds up Den Ridge; Caldwell Fork roars below. While climbing, you see many dead American chestnut stumps. The trail continues through mixed hardwoods, including red maple, chestnut oak, and some larger Eastern hemlocks. At approximately **1.8** mile, you may see Fraser magnolia and sourwood. Sourwood trunks are usually curved and were the preferred wood for the runners of land sleds used by mountain folk. The trail enters a grove of large Eastern hemlock, then winds around a small ravine filled with younger hemlocks. To the left are partial views of Cataloochee Valley.

By now the trail is descending gradually. Soon you reach the site of Robert Palmer's former farm. According to purchase records, he owned a three-room log house, two-room log house, four-stall barn, apple house, and spring house on 255.5 acres. In 1929, when the land was purchased for the national park, "Booger" was paid $5,375.

After crossing Palmer Branch on a small log bridge at mile **2.4**, the trail heads slightly uphill through white pine and then a rich, mixed woodland of sizable Eastern hemlock, tuliptree, pignut hickory, and various oaks and maples. To the right a small spring-fed rivulet carves out the earth, slowly forming its own valley. If you're lucky, you might hear the drawn-out staccato call of the reclusive Yellow-billed Cuckoo, a New World member of the Cuckoo family.

At about **2.8** miles, curving around a level part of the ridge, you enter a rosebay rhododendron thicket and cross a series of five shallow spring-fed seeps which may show evidence of wallowing by wild hogs. At one point, there is a partial view of Cataloochee Divide, with Caldwell Fork barely audible below. Summer wildflowers in this stretch of trail include sundrops and larger purple-fringed orchids.

The trail continues through second-growth Eastern hemlocks, then heads downhill, weaving among rotting American chestnut. Northern maidenhair ferns grow on the right. To the left stands a huge twin-trunk tuliptree—actually two 6' diameter trunks stemming from the same root system. By **4.1** miles, you pass a stone wall. Approximately 100 yards long and 2' wide, this stacked stone wall has no mortar; yet it is so well-constructed it stands intact. Near the wall is a giant tuliptree, its hollow trunk so large that a person could stand inside it.

After rock-hopping across a large fast-moving fork of Snake Branch, you walk downstream among large hemlocks and tuliptrees. Soon you rock hop across Snake Branch where you see another stone wall; though the upper half is collapsing, the lower half is intact. A third wall appears to the right, this one heading away from the creek in an "L" shape. Then the trail reaches an opening of ox-eye daisy, daisy-fleabane, tall meadowrue, and dwarf cinquefoil. After another stream crossing, you enter a thicket of rosebay rhododendron, then emerge into a grassy clearing where a black walnut flourishes. A depression in the ground (to the left of the trail) marks the home site of Carson Messer; the notched American chestnut logs of his cabin are decaying.

At **4.7** miles the Boogerman Trail ends and you rejoin Caldwell Fork Trail. Turn to the right and follow the trail as it courses through rosebay rhododendron and dog-hobble, beneath Eastern hemlock and yellow birch, and soon remains the only opening in unbroken forest, rendering trailsides the only openings for new growth. Thus the banks teem with young trees competing for sunlight. The view varies; sometimes the mature forest is obscured by dense rosebay rhododendron and dog-hobble. Two other noteworthy features: 1) a large Fraser magnolia clump consisting of one main trunk and roughly 50 shoots all stemming from the same root system, and 2) further along, deep pools in Caldwell Fork framed by rock shelves and overhanging bushes—good trout habitat. In **6.7** miles, you reach the point where the trail first intersected with Boogerman Trail; look for a small waterfall in Caldwell Fork near this juncture.

Retrace your steps on Caldwell Fork Trail for another **0.8** mile until you reach your car.

CHARLIES BUNION & THE JUMPOFF

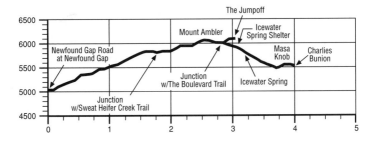

LENGTH: 8.0 miles roundtrip from Newfound Gap parking area to Charlies Bunion and back; 6.5 miles roundtrip from Newfound Gap parking area to the Jumpoff and back; 9.5 miles roundtrip from Newfound Gap parking area to the Jumpoff and Charlies Bunion and back.

HIGHLIGHTS: Spectacular views, spruce-fir forest.

CAUTIONS: Spur trail to Jumpoff is steep, rocky, eroded. Exposed cliffs on Bunion, Jumpoff. Route may be icy in winter.

MAP KEY: 8D; USGS quads: Mt. Le Conte, Clingmans Dome, Mt. Guyot.

USE: Hiking trail.

TRAILHEAD: Newfound Gap parking area at Newfound Gap, midway between Gatlinburg, TN and Cherokee, NC on Newfound Gap Road (U.S. 441).

Both of these places offer spectacular views. Though it is almost vertical, the Jumpoff is clothed with vegetation. Not so Charlies Bunion. It is as steep as the Jumpoff, but it is mostly bare rock. The two places are only about a mile apart, as the raven flies, and each can be seen from the other.

This doesn't mean you have to reach both on the same hike. They're presented together here because much of the trail is the same to both.

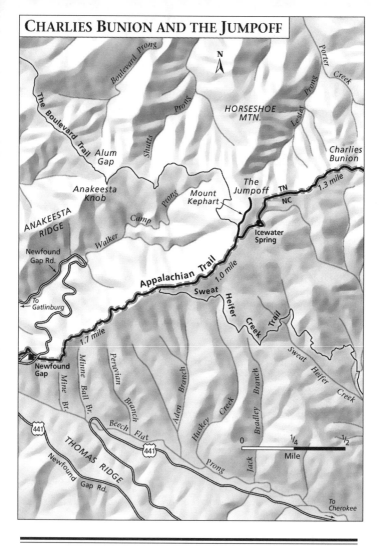

CHARLIES BUNION AND THE JUMPOFF

N

Porter Creek

HORSESHOE MTN.

Boulevard Prong

Shutts Prong

Lester Prong

The Boulevard Trail

Alum Gap

Anakeesta Knob

Camp Prong

Mount Kephart

The Jumpoff

Charlies Bunion

TN
NC

1.3 mile

ANAKEESTA RIDGE

Newfound Gap Rd.

To Gatlinburg

Walker Camp Prong

Appalachian Trail

Icewater Spring

1.0 mile

1.7 mile

Sweat Heifer Creek Trail

Newfound Gap

Sweat Heifer Creek

441

Mine Br.

Minne Ball Br.

THOMAS RIDGE

Newfound Gap Rd.

Peruvian Branch

Beech Flat

Aden Branch

Huskey Creek

Jack Branch

Bradley Branch

Kephart Prong

441

0   1/4   1/2
Mile

To Cherokee

Get on the Appalachian Trail near the interpretive sign at the upper end of the parking area and head eastward. You'll soon be away from the sound of automobiles and the smell of exhaust fumes, and you'll be walking through a forest of red spruce and fir trees, cool and dimly lighted on the hottest, brightest days.

Trees, flowers, ferns, mosses and lichens cover nearly every inch of ground except the trail. Rainfall is heavy. Rhododendron and other shrubs grow out of rock ledges where very little soil is visible.

However, nature is not always a constructive builder. Look a few miles northward at the great scars on the north slope of Mt. Le Conte. Most of these were left by a Labor Day weekend flash flood in 1951. It may be a century before nature's more gentle hand restores what she swept away here in one fierce hour.

Spruce and fir are found much more in Canada than in this latitude. The cool temperatures at the high-altitude crest of the Great Smokies permit their growth. Here's how to distinguish spruce from fir:

Spruce grows larger. It has short, sharp needles that are green all over. Fir has larger needles which are flat, green on top and white on the bottom. Spruce bark is scaly but fir bark is smooth. You'll see more moss on fir bark, because the scales drop off the spruce bark, carrying the moss with them. Fir bark is covered with small blisters.

A recent tragedy of the Great Smokies is that tiny creatures called balsam wooly adelgids have killed many of the park's mature Fraser fir trees since the insects were first detected in the park on Mt. Sterling in 1963.

You'll find flowers blooming along this trail any time between the frost seasons. One that's numerous in late summer is the touch-me-not, ranging in color from yellow to nearly white. Touch a touch-me-not seed pod and you'll find how it got its name. The pod bursts open and the seeds are scattered.

Two and seven-tenths miles east of Newfound Gap, the trail forks. The left fork is the Boulevard Trail, to Mt. Le Conte. The right one continues as the Appalachian Trail.

To reach the Jumpoff, take the Boulevard Trail for a few yards, looking, as you walk, for the marker that will put you on the narrow Jumpoff trail that angles to the right. It's a rough trail but not a dangerous one if you are reasonably careful.

You'll soon be going through a large blackberry patch. These high-mountain blackberry canes are virtually thornless. Their small, seedy berries ripen in late August or September.

From the blackberry thicket, the trail winds along a spruce-fir razorback ridge and reaches the Jumpoff. You'll see outcropping slate layers pointed skyward. Down to the right for a thousand feet there is nothing much but fresh air and a view.

Although the cliff wall plunges nearly straight down, it is clothed with shrubs and small trees. The small-leaved rhododendron (*Rhododendron minus*) seems to be the dominant cliffhanger.

If you're a bird watcher, don't forget your glasses on this trip. You'll see many small birds, including several warblers, flitting along almost directly below you. And you may see a raven or a hawk.

To go to Charlies Bunion, go back to (or continue on) the Appalachian Trail. A good resting place not far from The Boulevard trail junction is the new, improved AT shelter at Ice Water Spring.

Some of the fir trees near the shelter are healthy, and Park Service researchers are studying some stands in this area to see if some adelgid-resistant strains may exist.

Descend steadily through a gully caused by millions of footsteps and seven feet of yearly rain. Hikers along this stretch sound like teams of shod horses on cobblestones as they plod over slabs of silvery yellow slate and flaggy sandstone. Eight-tenths mile past the shelter, the trail leaves the red spruce, juvenile Fraser fir, and birch forest and changes abruptly to young second growth black cherry, yellow birch, American beech, and thornless blackberry. Swinging around from the shoulder of Mt. Kephart, the trail straddles the state line, and reaches a spectacular view of Charlies Bunion.

In 1925, before the park was established, a fire killed much of the vegetation on the peak that later was called Charlies Bunion. A flash flood hit the same area four years later. With the anchoring tree roots killed by the fire, the soil on the Tennessee side was washed away by the flood. Spectacular bare rock remains.

According to Paul Fink, in his "The Names and Lore of the Great Smokies," a group of North Carolinians hiked to the top of the

The view from Charlies Bunion.

mountain to see what damage the flood had done. In the group was Charlie Connor, a man who had long suffered from an unusually large bunion. Looking at the bare-rock knob, one of the others said, "That sticks out like Charlie's bunion."

CHESTNUT TOP & SCHOOLHOUSE GAP

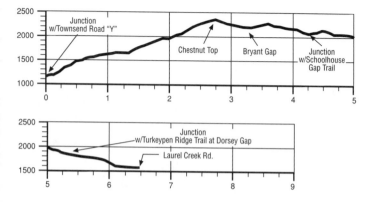

LENGTH: 6.4 miles one way from the Townsend "Y" to the Schoolhouse Gap Trailhead on Laurel Creek Road (the road to Cades Cove). A car shuttle is recommended.

HIGHLIGHTS: Early spring wildflowers.

MAP KEY: 4 D; USGS quads: Wear Cove, Kinzel Springs.

USE: Horse and hiking trail.

TRAILHEAD: Park at the Townsend "Y" (the intersection where the road from Townsend meets the road to Cades Cove). Chestnut Top Trail starts across the Townsend entrance road from the large parking area.

I've done this hike several times, but the time that remains most pleasant in my memory was on an April day when the wildflowers put on a show for me and my wife, Alberta, and anybody else who crossed Chestnut Top that day.

Though one sees occasional wildflowers all along the way, their thickest concentration is along the first three-quarter mile of Chestnut Top Trail, on the steep northeast-facing hillside above Little River, near the park entrance at Townsend.

We were on the trail well ahead of the blooms of laurel, rosebay

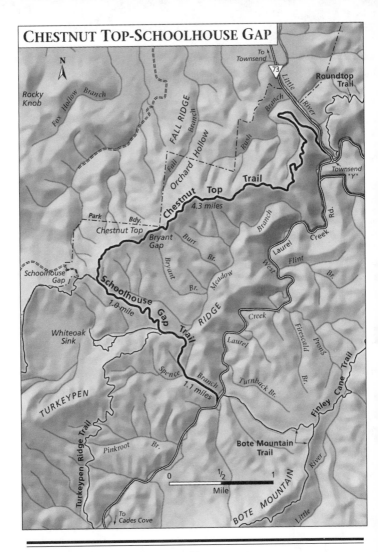

CHESTNUT TOP-SCHOOLHOUSE GAP

N

To Townsend

73

Roundtop Trail

Rocky Knob

Fox Hollow Branch

FALL RIDGE

Orchard Hollow Branch

Fall Branch

Rush Branch

Little River

Townsend "Y"

Chestnut Top Trail

4.3 miles

Park Bdy.

Chestnut Top

Bryant Gap

Burr Br.

Bryant Br.

Meadow Br.

Branch

Laurel Creek Rd.

Flint Br.

West

Schoolhouse Gap

Schoolhouse Gap Trail

1.0 mile

RIDGE

Creek

Laurel

Firescald Prong

Whiteoak Sink

Spence Branch

1.1 miles

Turnback Br.

Finley Cane Trail

TURKEYPEN

Turkeypen Ridge Trail

Pinkroot Br.

Bote Mountain Trail

0   1/2   1
Mile

To Cades Cove

BOTE MOUNTAIN

Little River

73

rhododendron, galax and even wild iris. But we were there the right week for dogwood, redbud, serviceberry, hepatica, spring beauty, bloodroot, trailing arbutus, bishop's cap, two varieties of trillium, four of violet and seven or eight other species of wildflowers.

In the first 20 to 30 minutes of your walk you'll be traveling northwesterly, in the same general direction as the river and the highway. But while the highway and the river gradually descend toward the village of Townsend, you'll be ascending sharply along the hillside.

This is a moist area, favorable to many wildflower species. Trillium, great chickweed, hepatica and bloodroot do especially well here. You'll reach a point where you have a good view of Townsend. Then you'll come to a crest where the trail turns abruptly southeastward.

Here, everything is different. It's dry, instead of moist. Pines and oaks predominate in the forest. You'll walk on soft pine needles much of the next several miles. Except for thickets of laurel, wildflowers are fewer and farther apart—an occasional halberd-leaved violet or birdfoot violet, an inconspicuous pipsissewa.

But it's pleasant walking up here on or near the crest of Chestnut Top Lead. Sometimes the trail ascends gently, at other times it descends just as gently. You get occasional glimpses of the main crest of the Great Smokies, miles eastward.

About 4.3 miles from where you started, you'll reach the Schoolhouse Gap Trail. Actually, it's an old road, built long before the national park was established, a segment of a road that travellers used to go from lowland Blount County to the crest of the Great Smokies at Spence Field.

I suggest that you turn left here. A walk of about two miles will take you to the Laurel Creek Road (the road to Cades Cove), where you should have arranged to have a car waiting for you. Otherwise, you'll have to walk the nearly four miles along Laurel Creek Road back to your car. Of course, a third option is to skip the Schoolhouse Gap Trail and retrace your steps on the Chestnut Top Trail, for a roundtrip hike of 8.6 miles.

← *Spring wildflowers along Schoolhouse Gap Trail.*

COOPER ROAD - GOLD MINE TRAIL

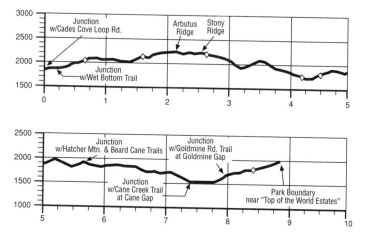

LENGTH: 8.8 miles one way from Cades Cove Loop Road to Top o' the World development at park boundary. A car shuttle is recommended.

HIGHLIGHTS: Historic road, wildflowers.

MAP KEY: 2-3 D; USGS quads: Blockhouse, Kinzel Spring.

USE: Horse and hiking trail.

TRAILHEAD: See narrative below.

To start at the eastern end of the hike, drive the one-way Cades Cove Loop Road 4.2 miles from its beginning to the Cooper Road Trail trailhead at sign post #9.

To start this hike at the western end, leave Foothills Parkway at Look Rock and drive 2.2 miles down road into Top 0' The World development. This brings you to an old unimproved road which leads to your right down to the park boundary. Park your car at the first convenient place on the old road, for it is too rough for most vehicles except Jeeps. This is Gold Mine Trail. Follow it 0.8 mile to where it

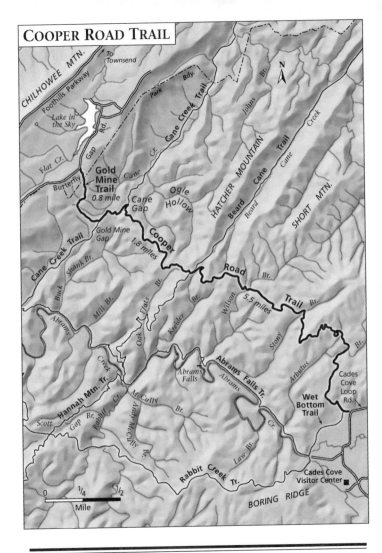

COOPER ROAD TRAIL

CHILHOWEE MTN.

Foothills Parkway

To Townsend

Lake in the Sky

Gap Rd.

Park Bdy.

Cane Creek Trail

Flat Cr.

Butterfly

Cane

Gold Mine Trail
0.8 mile

Cane Gap

Ogle Hollow

Johns Br.

N

Cane Creek

HATCHER MOUNTAIN

Beard

Cane Trail

Beard

SHORT MTN.

Cane Creek Trail

Gold Mine Gap

Buck Shank Br.

Cooper
1.8 miles

Abrams

Mill Br.

Oak Flats

Kreider Br.

Wilson

Br.

Road

Br.

Stony

Trail
5.5 miles

Br.

Creek

Hannah Mtn. Tr.

McCully Br.

Abrams Falls

Abrams

Abrams Falls Tr.

Cr.

Arbutus

Br.

Cades Cove Loop Rd.

Wet Bottom Trail

Scott

Gap Br.

Rabbit Cr.

Andy McCully Br.

Law Br.

Rabbit Creek Tr.

Cades Cove Visitor Center

BORING RIDGE

0   ¼   ½
Mile

joins Cooper Road and continue left on Cooper.

Most persons will find this hike too long as a round-tripper. So you should arrange to have a car waiting at the end of a one-way hike.

This is an excellent early-spring hike, when trailing arbutus blooms. Cooper Road crosses Arbutus Ridge, aptly named for the little trailing plants with leathery leaves and sweet-smelling flowers that grow on it in unusual abundance. Cardinal flowers grow near the small streams and brighten this hike in early autumn.

A few Eastern red cedars grow here. These evergreens, so abundant elsewhere in Tennessee, are uncommon within the park boundaries. They grow at low elevation and usually on limestone, which underlies the sandstone of the ridges that you have been climbing. Redbud, which blooms in March and April and has smooth, heart-shaped leaves, also grows along this road because of the same conditions.

Oldtimers say this was the first road from Cades Cove to Maryville. There is evidence that Indians used the route prior to the arrival of settlers of European descent. Cove dwellers traveled it on foot, by horseback and in wagons and buggies. Daniel David Foute, an early settler who owned much of the cove, improved the road in the 1830s for wagon transport to Maryville. The James Carson Iron Works, built on Kingfisher Creek in the 1830s, depended on the road, and Cades Cove farmers shipped apples, livestock, honey, lumber, and other products. It was a two-day drive with a herd of cattle to market in Maryville.

Miners found gold in small quantities near what is now the western boundary of the park. Thus, the name of the old road on the western end of the hike.

CUCUMBER GAP LOOP

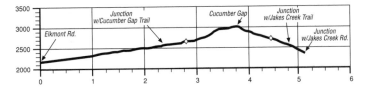

LENGTH: 5.5-mile-long loop hike (including 0.4 mile of road walking not shown on elevation profile).
HIGHLIGHTS: Easy trail, spring wildflowers, beautiful river.
CAUTIONS: One unbridged stream crossing that can be difficult in very high water.
MAP KEY: 6 C-D; USGS quads: Gatlinburg, Silers Bald.
USE: Hiking trail.
TRAILHEAD: Drive to Elkmont Campground 4.9 miles west of Sugarlands Visitor Center. Just before the campground entrance station, turn left. Little River trailhead is 0.6 mile up the side road at the gate and trail sign.

This is one of the most delightful short hikes in the Great Smokies. Wildflowers bloom along it in great numbers in spring. It has no high hills. It connects Little River, on the east, with Jakes Creek, on the West.

Little River Trail starts at a locked gate and proceeds up a gravel road along the river. For half a mile the road runs between unoccupied Elkmont cabins. These vacation homes were constructed prior to park establishment and their future is the subject of some controversy between those favoring historic preservation and those hoping to see the area restored to its wild, pre-settlement condition. The buildings are off limits, but deer, bear, and Wild Turkey can not read the signs and may be seen in the yards. In mid-June, this area is famous for its light show performed by synchronous fireflies.

Little River is actually pretty big. It drains a large area of the

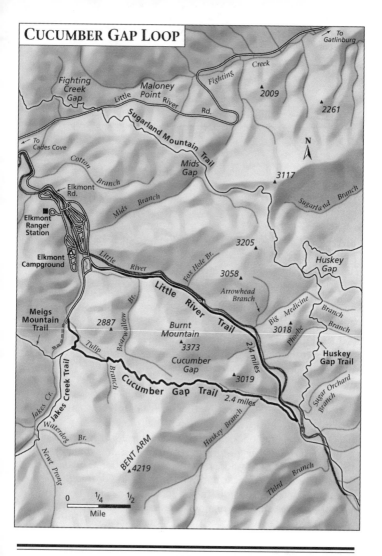

CUCUMBER GAP LOOP

To Gatlinburg

Fighting Creek

Fighting Creek Gap

Maloney Point

Little River Rd.

2009

2261

Sugarland Mountain Trail

To Cades Cove

Cotton Branch

Mids Gap

3117

Elkmont Rd.

Mids Branch

Sugarland Branch

Elkmont Ranger Station

Elkmont Campground

Little River

3205

3058

Fox Hole Br.

Huskey Gap

Arrowhead Branch

Big Medicine Branch

Little River Trail

Branch

Meigs Mountain Trail

Bearwallow Br.

2887

Burnt Mountain 3373

3018

Phoebe

Huskey Gap Trail

Tulip Branch

Cucumber Gap

2.4 miles

3019

Sugar Orchard branch

Jakes Cr.

Jakes Creek Trail

Cucumber Gap Trail

2.4 miles

Huskey Branch

Waterdog Br.

Newt Prong

BENT ARM
4219

Third Branch

0   1/4   1/2
Mile

Tennessee side of the Smokies, carries a lot of water, and has branches from the highest ridges. Over millions of years, Little River carved out a wide valley that leads right to the base of the Smokies' crest, and it was this easy access that attracted Little River Lumber Company.

The company bought out the few farms and built a base camp with a sawmill at Elkmont. Then crews moved up the rivers and branches with road and rail lines, set up temporary camps, cut all the trees, and moved on. Rail lines went up steep areas such as Rough Creek and Goshen Prong, and when the terrain was too steep even for the railroads, loggers pulled the logs down with overhead cable skidders, mule teams, or wooden chutes. In extreme cases, men ball-hooted the logs—they cleared an area below where the logs had been cut and rolled or shot them down the steep hillsides toward a rail siding. This was dangerous work and made even worse gashes in the mountains than routine logging. Evidence of logging can still be found along the road; look for cables, pullies, and railroad ties.

In the late 1920s, Little River Lumber Company agreed to sell its large holdings to park organizers only if it could continue logging for five years. As a result of the sale agreement, the park was established in 1934 even though the company continued to lay track and clear-cut virgin timber until 1938. Though it is sad we cannot see the magnificent virgin forests, a new, beautiful forest now fills this area.

Beyond the cabins, the trail enters woods and reaches some house-sized boulders. The wet rocks on the right harbor mosses, liverworts, and walking fern, and many wildflowers grow at the base of the rocks. In mid-summer look for Ruby-throated Hummingbirds feeding on the nectar of crimson bee balm, also known as Oswego tea.

At mile **1.4**, there is a bench and a big, deep, green pool. A little farther is another bench with a view of rapids on a curve of Little River. Notice a bunch of yellow birch trees just up-trail from the bench with their bark curled in perfect ringlets. On the right is a patch of umbrella leaf, a wildflower with dinner-plate-sized leaves on stalks about 18" tall. This plant is related to may-apple and is uncommon, growing only in wet rocky places like this. It blooms in April or May, and the leaves last until late fall.

At mile **2.4**, Cucumber Gap Trail merges with Little River Trail and is marked by a bench at the base of a big sycamore. Follow Cucumber Gap Trail up a gentle ascent through a large grove of second growth tuliptrees, more evidence of the Little River Lumber Company operations. Large banks on the lower part of the trail indicate that it was an old logging road or railroad bed. Park records show that the route was rebuilt as a trail by the Civilian Conservation Corps in the 1930s, connecting it to the Jakes Creek watershed.

At mile **2.7**, the trail crosses the first prominent landmark, Huskey Branch, which is easily forded on numerous flat stepping stones, unless there have been recent heavy rains. After Huskey Branch, the forest understory remains thick with small Eastern hemlock and rosebay rhododendron. In early spring, the entire trail shows off blooms of trout-lily, spring-beauty, bloodroot, Fraser sedge, and trillium. In summer, the undergrowth at the path's edge becomes thick with dog-hobble, cinnamon ferns and Christmas ferns. Before the trail approaches Cucumber Gap, it crosses two small unnamed branches and several low and damp run-off areas, which in July and August are scattered with patches of scarlet bee-balm. Also, watch for the deer which frequent this area.

Near the top of the gap are a large number of Fraser magnolias, sometimes called "cucumber trees," for which the gap and the trail are probably named. In truth, the cucumber tree is a separate species, *Magnolia acuminata*, but both trees grow a long, bumpy fruit which bears a certain resemblance to a cucumber. Interestingly, hikers say that in May and June patches of Indian cucumber root (*Medeola virginiana*) can be observed on this trail, suggesting another origin for the unusual name.

At the gap (mile **3.8**), the trail provides a partial vista in late fall and winter of Burnt Mountain (3,373') and the narrow valley created by Bear Wallow Creek. Violets, hepatica, cut-leaved toothwort, and other wildflowers bloom here in spring. At this point the trail makes a gradual, easy descent and levels off into a forest of tuliptrees, mountain maple, hemlock, and basswood trees. Winding through these trees is a great deal of wild grapevine, some as large as six inches in diameter and climbing more than 100 feet into the forest canopy.

Majestic and boisterous Pileated Woodpeckers seem to frequent this area. Also look for pink turtleheads in bloom during August and September.

About a half-mile after the gap, look for a flat area in the valley below (to the right). This large clearing was owned by Bill Teaster, who had a small cabin on the site and cultivated crops on about 12 of his 41.5 acres. Park archives suggest that Teaster did not want to sell his land to the state commission, which purchased land for the national park. The surveyor, who had estimated the value of the land at $15 per acre, asked Teaster what he thought it was worth, and he said it was worth twice that amount. The case was settled in court in 1930; Teaster received $17.50 per acre and a "lifetime lease." To expedite cases like this one, the federal government offered older residents the opportunity to stay on their land as renters (at a very low rate) until their deaths.

As the trail descends toward the Jakes Creek Trail, it crosses Tulip Branch, called Poplar Branch by the original residents of the area. Both names have as their origin the extremely large tuliptrees that grew along the branch here at the turn of the century. "Uncle" Jim Shelton, who helped build the first railroads into the Elkmont area, recalled seeing a tuliptree so large that it "took two flat cars to carry it out of the mountains." At present there are still many two- and three-foot diameter tuliptrees to admire along this section of the trail.

The Cucumber Gap Trail ends at the Jakes Creek Trail, which also follows the route of an old logging railroad. To return to your car, turn right on Jakes Creek Trail and follow it to the trailhead (0.3 mile). Then descend on the road among the old summer homes (go right at the fork) and walk 0.4 mile to the Little River Trailhead.

GABES MOUNTAIN TRAIL

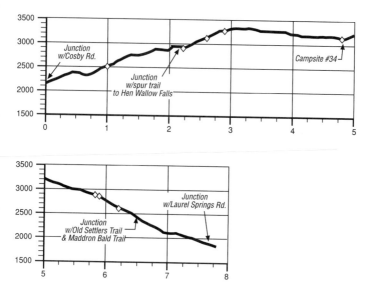

LENGTH: 4.2 miles roundtrip from Cosby Campground to Hen wallow Falls and back; 7.8 miles one-way from Cosby Campground to the Maddron Bald trailhead near Highway 321 and Yogi's Campground (car shuttle recommended).

HIGHLIGHTS: Hen Wallow Falls, old-growth forest.

CAUTIONS: Slippery rocks at falls, some slippery stream crossings in high water.

MAP KEY: 9-10 B; USGS quads: Hartford, Luftee Knob, Mt. Guyot, Jones Cove.

USE: Hiking trail.

TRAILHEAD: Park at the hiker parking area just before the entrance station for Cosby Campground (by the picnic area). Walk back across the road you drove in on to find Gabes Mountain Trail.

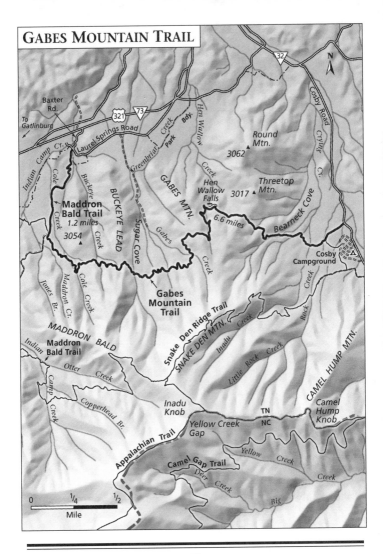

GABES MOUNTAIN TRAIL

N

To Gatlinburg

Baxter Rd.

321 73

Laurel Springs Road

Indian Camp Cr.

Cole Creek

Buckeye Creek

BUCKEYE LEAD

Greenbriar Creek

Park Bdy.

Hen Wallow Creek

GABES MTN.

Round Mtn. 3062

Cosby Road

Crying Cr.

Threetop Mtn.

Hen Wallow Falls 3017

6.6 miles

Bearneck Cove

Maddron Bald Trail
1.2 miles
3054

Sugar Cove

Gabes Creek

Cole Creek

Maddron Cr.

Jones Br.

Gabes Mountain Trail

Cosby Campground

Rock Creek

MADDRON BALD

Maddron Bald Trail

Snake Den Ridge Trail

SNAKE DEN MTN.

Inadu Creek

Little Rock Creek

CAMEL HUMP MTN.

Indian

Camp Creek

Otter Creek

Copperhead Br.

Inadu Knob

Yellow Creek Gap

TN
NC

Camel Hump Knob

Appalachian Trail

Camel Gap Trail

Deer Creek

Yellow Creek

Big Creek

0   1/4   1/2
Mile

85

This hike on the Gabes Mountain Trail will take you through historic land where mountain farmers and orchard keepers lived for generations before the area became part of the National Park. The wilderness has reclaimed most of it, but you will still see many lasting reminders of those who once lived, labored and loved on this stony land.

Gabes Mountain Trail twists up and over small ridges and crosses several small streams on picturesque footlogs. After about a mile you reach an intersection with an old road. Your trail turns abruptly left here. Another quarter-mile brings you atop the spine of a ridge and a left turn in the trail. Look a few yards back to your right and you will see Sally Sutton's grave.

The first time I saw this lonely grave in the forest, it had both headstone and footstone. The headstone bore Sally Sutton's name. No dates. Now, the headstone is gone; only the footstone remains. People who know the area told me that she was Sally Grooms Sutton, second of Jim Sutton's three wives. The family once lived not far from this spot. She often worked in the fields nearby. She once told her husband she thought the place was pretty and that she would like to be buried here.

He remembered her wish.

Bill Barnes operated an apple orchard near where Sally Sutton rests, Edgar Williamson, a former resident of the area, told me. He said he and others used to take 50-pound bran sacks into the nearby woods in autumn and fill them with chestnuts. He remembered picking wild strawberries on a hill where rhododendron and hemlock now grow.

Hen Wallow Falls is about 60 feet high. You reach it by way of a steep side trail that plunges down about 700 feet from the Gabes Mountains Trail. Be careful going down this trail when it's covered with snow or ice.

On a morning in late spring, I once saw the stone face of Hen Wallow Falls covered with hundreds of salamanders. Most of them rested in only a thin film of water, away from the main force of the falling water. I never learned the reason for such a splendid salamander congregation. In deep winter, I've seen the falls almost totally covered with ice.

For a long time, I erroneously presumed that Hen Wallow Falls was so named because domestic chickens once had a wallow near it. But another Williamson—Bill, who lives in Cosby—finally told me the straight but bizarre story:

In an unnamed small community lived a family which one spring ordered 100 baby chicks from a hatchery. They hoped most of the 100 would grow up to be egg-laying hens. The family would eat some of the eggs and sell the rest. But that's not what happened. When the chickens became old enough for their gender to be obvious, the family counted about 95 roosters and five pullets. People in a nearby community, also without a name, thought this was pretty funny. They began calling the other community Roostertown. Naturally, the people of Roostertown did not appreciate being called Roostertowners. So they struck back. They called the other community Hen Wallow. There was no basis at all for this; it was out of pure revenge. But the name stuck to Hen Wallow Falls and Hen Wallow Creek. They're on most Great Smokies maps. But Roostertown is not on Great Smokies maps. However, when you drive on Highway 321, a short distance west of Cosby, you will notice a marker for Roostertown Road.

Back to the Gabes Mountain Trail. You soon cross Lower Falling Branch, a major tributary of Hen Wallow. Then you follow the trail sharply south up the mountain and cross the same stream again, going back east this time. Farther up the mountain, you swing west again and cross Lower Falling Branch the last time. There also is an Upper Falling Branch, but the trail does not cross it.

Another Williamson, Olie, said his grandparents, John and Elvira Williamson, moved into a house above Upper Falling Branch in 1898. He said his grandfather had to carry their cook stove on his back.

The next few miles are pleasant. You see long stretches of rhododendron. Then a long strip of partridge berry, the ground-hugging little evergreen. The forest at this elevation was cut over only lightly, if at all. The hemlock is the dominant tree species and some of them are huge and lovely. You'll also see big yellow buckeyes and tuliptrees.

Finally—after crossing small streams named Gabes, Greenbrier, Buckeye and Cole—you reach the Maddron Bald Trail, which actually is a road at this point. Turn right on it and follow it north to the one-room log house built by Willis Baxter in 1889. Baxter built his house of chestnut, from sills to shingles. But because of the death of the chestnut trees, park maintenance people have had to replace some of the chestnut material with other kinds of wood. Note that the house is entirely windowless.

If you have a second car waiting for you at the end of this hike, walk about a mile on down the Maddron Bald Trail to the park boundary and then turn onto Baxter Road to Highway 321. This trailhead has a problem. Thieves have taken some hikers' cars. Vandals have damaged others. The last time I made the hike, my hiking buddy and I left one car at Ledford's Market, on Highway 321, about two-tenths of a mile west of Laurel Springs Road. The market sometimes charges a small parking fee.

← *Hen Wallow Falls.*

GRAPEYARD RIDGE TRAIL

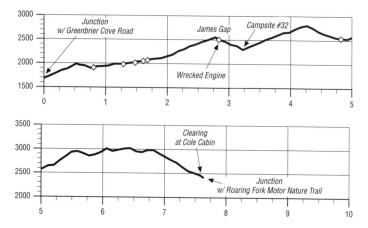

LENGTH: 7.6 miles one way from Greenbrier Cove to Roaring Fork Motor Nature Trail. A car shuttle is recommended.

HIGHLIGHTS: Historic sites.

CAUTIONS: Unbridged stream crossings.

MAP KEY: 8-7 C; USGS quad: Mt. Le Conte

USE: Horse and hiking trail.

TRAILHEAD: Drive to the Greenbrier entrance to the national park 5.9 miles east of Gatlinburg on U.S. 321. Continue past the ranger station and the first picnic area to the junction of the road to Ramsey Cascade Trail and the road to Porters Creek Trail. Park on the left, just before the bridge. Grapeyard Ridge Trail starts on the right.

The first thing to do on this hike is get over the first small ridge, after which walking becomes easier and viewing more interesting. Park your car on the side of the road near the river just below the confluence of Porters Creek and Middle Prong of the Little Pigeon. The trail takes off up the bank on the opposite side of the road.

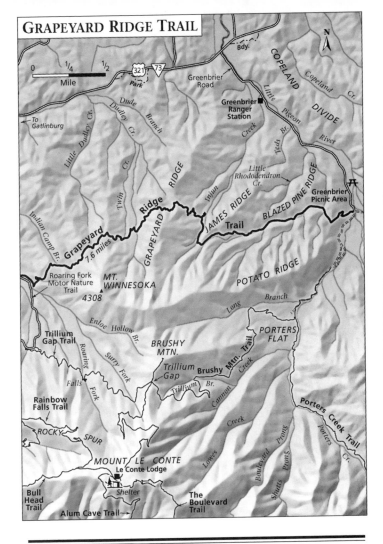

GRAPEYARD RIDGE TRAIL

0   1/4   1/2
Mile

Bdy.

COPELAND DIVIDE

Copeland Cr.

Park 321 73

Greenbrier Road

Greenbrier Ranger Station

Little Pigeon River

Teds Br.

Greenbrier Creek

To Gatlinburg

Dude Branch

Little Dudley Cr.

Dudley Cr.

Twin Cr.

GRAPEYARD RIDGE

Little Rhododendron Cr.

JAMES RIDGE

Wijun

BLAZED PINE RIDGE

Greenbrier Picnic Area

Grapeyard Ridge
7.6 miles

Indian Camp Br.

Trail

Roaring Fork Motor Nature Trail

MT. WINNESOKA
4308

POTATO RIDGE

Long Branch

Enloe Hollow Br.

PORTERS FLAT

Trillium Gap Trail

Surry Fork

BRUSHY MTN.

Roaring Fork

Trillium Gap

Brushy Mtn. Trail

Cannon Creek

Falls

Trillium Br.

Rainbow Falls Trail

ROCKY SPUR

Creek

Lowes Creek

Porters Creek Trail

Boulevard Prong

Shutts Prong

Porters Cr.

MOUNT LE CONTE

Le Conte Lodge

Shelter

Bull Head Trail

Alum Cave Trail→

The Boulevard Trail

(Unless you intend to do a rather long roundtrip, you should earlier have left another car at the end of the hike, near stop #10 on Roaring Fork Motor Nature Trail, on the left side of the road, three miles from the beginning of the motor trail.)

After you top the first hill, within 10 to 15 minutes, you'll be walking down into the delightful valley of Rhododendron Creek. It hasn't always been Rhododendron Creek. Before the area became part of the National Park, this stream was Big Laurel Creek. But because the park had too many creeks named "Laurel," park officials changed the names of all but one of them.

By whatever name you call it, this little valley is beautiful. You soon cross a small tributary of Rhododendron Creek and then you follow the trail for five crossings of the creek, as the trail and creek swap sides during a pleasant meander of about a mile. The narrow bottomland in summer is covered thickly with tall weeds and sparse tree growth. Joe Pye weeds wave pink-gray blooms 10 feet above ground, and you can guess that corn also grew tall here when farmers cultivated the rich bottomland. I picked big juicy blackberries here on a July morning.

Later, after I left the creek and started up James Ridge, I picked bear huckleberries. You reach the top of James Ridge at James Gap and start down into the valley of Injun Creek. Within two or three minutes after you leave the gap, you reach the creek.

And there, just a few feet below the crossing, lies an old sawmill steam engine that's been there since it wrecked in about 1920. The story told by Great Smokies oldtimers is that the engine had been used in Big Laurel (now Rhododendron) in sawing lumber for a new school in Greenbrier Cove. The job was finished and the steam engine was headed home. Up it went over James Gap. The intent was to drive it down Injun Creek and to the driver's home on Webb Creek. But the driver got too close to the edge and the engine toppled into the creek. The owner of the engine, Art Shultz, later had two wagonloads of salvaged material hauled away. But he did not salvage what you now see left in the creek. It is said to have been the first steam engine to come into the Greenbrier area that was able to propel itself with its steam, as well as power a saw with it.

Because "engine" when spoken sounds similar to "Injun," there are those who think the 'Injun" they see on the map as the name of the creek really should be "Engine," with the creek named for the wrecked steam engine. Others argue that it was Injun Creek before the engine wrecked. They believe that name was given the creek because there is an Indian graveyard beside the creek, approximately half way between the Grapeyard Ridge Trail and the Greenbrier ranger's residence beside the creek.

Follow the trail down parallel with the creek for 10 minutes to an intersection. The trail to the right goes about 100 yards to Campsite 32. Your trail is to the left, up Grapeyard Ridge. But before you take it, you may want to walk the other trail down to the campsite. Opposite the campsite is the site of an old home, marked by stone walls, an old zinc tub and a thick growth of poison ivy. Back to your trail.

You soon see a few old fence posts to the right of the trail, which was a country road when those posts were new. The highest point of this segment is the top of the ridge, about 2,800 feet, after which it's nearly all down hill to Dudley Creek. Lots of wild iris grows near the creek. So does crimson bee balm and tall phlox.

Just beyond the creek and mostly on the upper side of the trail notice the impressive stone walls. It was here that Levi Evans Ogle bought about 400 acres of old-growth-forest land in the early 1880s and turned much of it into an apple orchard. One of his granddaughters, Iva Ogle Wright, who was born nearby, recalls attending Dudley Creek School, which stood on a ridge between Dudley and Little Dudley Creeks. The teacher boarded with the Ogles. Iva Wright says her father, Coy Ogle, and her grandfather hauled wagonloads of apples to Knoxville to sell. They also hauled chestnuts to Knoxville. It is Mrs. Wright's memory that the apple orchard was still producing apples when the land was bought from her uncle, Ashley Ogle, for the park.

The trail splits a few yards down the creek from the Ogle home-site, with the right fork leading down to a riding stable. Yours is the left fork, on toward Roaring Fork, a little more than 2.5 miles away. Sometimes, especially during wet weather, the trail is not particularly pleasant from this point westward. Horses use it. They cut it up and muddy it.

The wildflower blooms sometimes are good enough to make you forget the mud. Look for mountain pepper-bush, crimson bee balm, coreopsis, yellow fringed orchids, phlox, rosebay rhododendron, violets and lots of wild iris in their seasons.

The first small stream west of Dudley Creek is one of its tributaries, Twin Creek. Then comes Little Dudley, and, a half-hour later, Indian Camp Branch. Soon after Indian Camp comes a trail fork. The trail to the left links up with the Trillium Gap Trail. Yours is to the right, only 5 to 10 minutes from where your waiting car should be parked on the Roaring Fork Motor Nature Trail.

But just before you reach the road, you'll want to pause and look at the old Jim Bales place: A log barn, corn crib and one-room cabin, all preserved by the Park Service. The cabin was moved from elsewhere in the park.

LAUREL FALLS - COVE MOUNTAIN

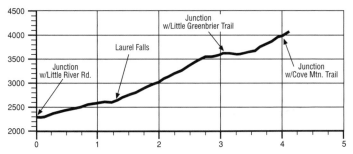

LENGTH: 2.6 miles roundtrip to Laurel Falls and back; 8.2 miles roundtrip to the top of Cove Mountain and back.

HIGHLIGHTS: Waterfall, big trees.

CAUTIONS: Do not climb on rocks around waterfall.

MAP KEY: 5-6 C; USGS quad: Gatlinburg.

USE: Hiking trail.

TRAILHEAD: the large parking area at Fighting Creek Gap, between Sugarlands Visitor Center and Elkmont Campground on the Little River Road.

Most persons who start this hike—from Fighting Creek Gap, on the Little River Road—walk only the 1.3 miles to spectacular Laurel Creek Falls. But in stopping there, they miss seeing a magnificent old-growth forest that begins less than a mile above the waterfall.
So popular is the short hike to the waterfall that the National Park Service has had to pave the trail to prevent erosion.

Along the first section of trail grows second-growth forest in which oaks and pines predominate. Growing under the oaks and pines much of the way is a thick stand of laurel, along with a sparse scattering of flame azalea. At this altitude, both usually bloom in late May. Low-growing trailing arbutus, wintergreen and galax also grow here, and the leaves of the wintergreen and galax often change from green to a lovely red or bronze by late winter.

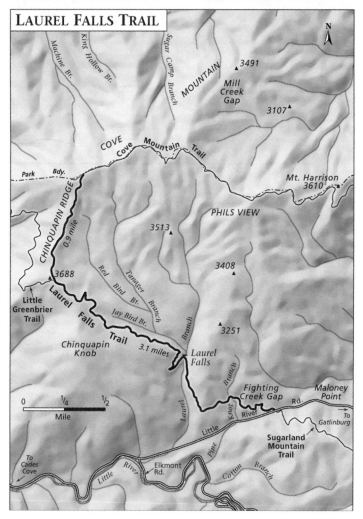

LAUREL FALLS TRAIL

Machine Br.

King Hollow Br.

Sugar Camp Branch

MOUNTAIN ▲ 3491

Mill Creek Gap

3107 ▲

COVE Cove Mountain Trail

Park Bdy.

CHINQUAPIN RIDGE

Mt. Harrison 3610 ▲

PHILS VIEW

3513 ▲

0.9 mile

3688

Little Greenbrier Trail

Laurel Falls Trail

Red Bird Br.

Trasger Branch

Jay Bird Br.

Chinquapin Knob

3.1 miles

3408 ▲

Branch

3251 ▲

Laurel Falls

Fighting Creek Gap

Maloney Point

Rd.

To Gatlinburg

Knob Branch

Laurel Branch

Little River

Sugarland Mountain Trail

0   ¼   ½
Mile

To Cades Cove

Little River

Elkmont Rd.

Pine Branch

Cotton Branch

Laurel Branch is one wild waterfall after another from high in the mountain almost to the point where it enters Little River. Laurel Falls is the most spectacular of its many jumps. The trail crosses the stream on a footbridge at about the middle of the split-level waterfall.

The trail is unpaved above the waterfall. And within less than a mile one enters a forest of giant tuliptrees and hemlocks. Loggers never cut this forest and the major reason is said to be that the area was too rugged for timber cutters to snake out the logs with horses.

A good time to make this hike is in late winter. With the leaves gone from the trees, it is easier to see the big tree trunks rising from the forest floor. Not all of them are rising. Countless fallen trunks lie in artistic haphazardness, in various stages of decay. Many are strikingly marked by green moss growing on top of them. Occasionally, one finds one in such advanced decay that ferns, wildflowers and small trees grow from it.

The tuliptree-hemlock forest lasts less than a mile. The trail, gently meandering near the crest of Chinquapin Ridge, next enters a forest where oaks grow again. But unlike the oak forest below the waterfall, this one up here has few pines. Red maple probably is the most abundant tree after the oaks.

This also is old-growth forest. But, generally, the oaks and maples aren't as large as the hemlocks and tulip poplars. However, you'll see a few large white oaks.

A tree that grows with the oaks and maples, as well as with the tulip poplars and hemlocks, is the silverbell. It has lovely white bell-shaped flowers in late April and May.

Near the top of the mountain, the trail intersects an old road. Turn left on the road and within about 150 yards, you'll reach an old fire tower at the top of Cove Mountain. From the top of the tower, it once was possible to see a long portion of the main range of the Great Smokies, to the south. But the tower now is an air quality monitoring station and the top is closed to the public.

However, here and there along the trail, one still can get good views of smaller portions of the main range.

PORTERS CREEK TRAIL

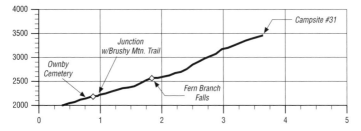

LENGTH: 3.6 miles roundtrip from Greenbrier Road to Fern Branch Falls and back; 7.2 miles roundtrip from Greenbrier Road to Campsite #31 and back.

HIGHLIGHTS: Wildflowers, waterfall.

MAP KEY: 8 C; USGS quad: Mt. Le Conte.

USE: Hiking trail.

TRAILHEAD: Take US 321 5.9 miles east of Gatlinburg, TN and turn onto the Greenbrier road at the park entrance sign. Pass the ranger station and two picnic areas. At mile 4.1, park on a traffic loop and look for the gate and trail sign.

Greenbrier Cove was heavily settled, and the established farmers and selective logging saved this area from big logging companies. In the early 1800s, the Whaley family is thought to have migrated from North Carolina through Dry Sluice Gap and found this sheltered, fertile valley. By the end of that century, 26 families lived here and, at one point, sent 225 children to the local school, which stood on the site of the present ranger station. The cove had four grist mills, three cemeteries, two churches, two stores, and two blacksmith shops. In 1925, Kimsey Whaley and James West Whaley built the two-story Greenbrier Hotel where Porters Creek joins the Middle Prong near the present picnic area. By this time, there were so many Whaleys in Greenbrier Cove that they needed distinctive nicknames such as Booger Bill, Whiteheaded Bill, and Humpy John.

This trail is famous for its wildflower displays in April and May. If

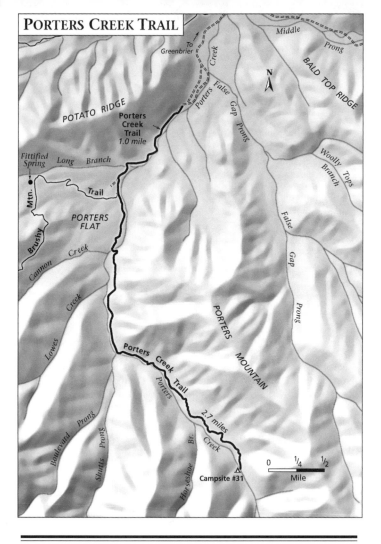

PORTERS CREEK TRAIL

Middle Prong

BALD TOP RIDGE

To Greenbrier

Porters Creek

False Gap Prong

N

POTATO RIDGE

Porters Creek Trail 1.0 mile

Woolly Tops Branch

Fittified Spring

Long Branch

Trail

Mtn.

PORTERS FLAT

Brushy

Cannon Creek

Lowes Creek

Creek

False Gap Prong

PORTERS MOUNTAIN

Porters Creek Trail

Porters

Boulevard Prong

Shutts Prong

Horseshoe Br.

Creek

2.7 miles

Campsite #31

0   1/4   1/2
Mile

you like to keep lists of what you see in bloom, you might get 30-40 species here. Consequently, the trail gets a fair amount of use. But there is plenty of parking near the trailhead.

After the gate, the trail rises gently. On the moist bank look for a variety of ferns, including Christmas, fragile, grape, silvery glade, maidenhair, lady, beech, and hay-scented. At mile **0.4**, the foundation of the Cantwell house stands on the right and the John Whaley house and farm site is across the creek. Solomon's seal, showy orchis, and poison ivy grow along the stone steps up to a house site, and there is a large patch of wood betony at the top. Other house sites, stone walls, and spring house foundations can be seen along this trail.

The trail crosses Long Branch on a good bridge at **0.7** mile. Up the hill from the bridge, look for a large patch of crested dwarf iris, the Tennessee state wildflower, on the left. They bloom in April and the leaves stay green for the rest of the spring and summer. Then on the right, you will see cement block steps up the bank to the Ownby Cemetery. The gravestones date from the early 1900s, but the families still maintain this cemetery and occasionally place new headstones. There is a skeleton of an old car to the right of the trail just beyond the cemetery.

The old road ends in Porters Flat, the open area where the Whaleys first settled. The Brushy Mountain Trail and the historic farm site are to the right and the Porters Creek Trail goes left.

Porters Creek Trail is narrow but easy walking. It descends through a forest of large Eastern hemlocks and Fraser magnolias to the creek. Painted trillium blooms here in late April. The creek itself is deep and rushing, tumbling over great boulders. At mile **1.5** you will cross on a very long, paved, foot log that is ingeniously perched on two boulders with little cement platforms to make it level.

Shortly after the foot log, you step into a different world—a moist, sheltered cove with massive yellow buckeye trees and flowers carpeting the ground between them. In early-to-mid April, the fringed phacelia look like a new snowfall. Through a hand lens, each phacelia flower looks like a snowflake. Toothwort, trillium, spring-beauty, hepatica, bloodroot, blue cohosh, phlox, bishop's cap, foamflower—this is just the beginning of the flower list for Porters Creek. The trail

April wildflowers along Porters Creek Trail.

turns right and ascends evenly, and as you go up, new flowers in each section brush against your ankles.

Soon the trail is high above the creek on your right, and you pass rock faces on the left. At this level you can find Dutchman's pipe vine, wild ginger, speckled wood lily, and Indian pink, all blooming in May or June. As the trail levels at **1.8** miles, a tiny creek crosses it after plunging and sliding over a 40' waterfall called Fern Branch Falls. Look to your left to see it. Watch for wild ginger and brook lettuce on the creek bank. A steep, nettle-lined side trail leads up to the waterfall, and a large fallen tree makes a good viewing spot.

If you proceed on Porters Creek Trail beyond the falls, the trail runs along a bench high above the creek. You will see black cohosh (which blooms in June or July and persists until September), plantain-leaved sedge, and more speckled wood lily. But as the trail rises, there are more Eastern hemlocks, and the wildflowers are replaced by a lush moss and fern ground cover. Fraser magnolias and yellow buckeyes grow among the hemlocks. The creek and the trail converge, and you can glimpse cascades and crystal pools. Note the big log jams created by flash floods which frequently roar down from the steep headwaters of this drainage.

At mile **3.6**, the trail turns right toward the creek and comes to the Campsite #31 signpost. A small spring just left of the signpost supplies water most of the year, and the pleasant campsite is ahead.

RAINBOW FALLS

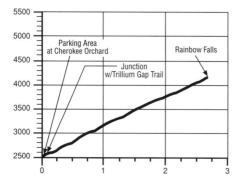

LENGTH: 5.6 miles roundtrip, from Rainbow Falls Parking Area on the Cherokee Orchard Road to Rainbow Falls and back.
HIGHLIGHTS: Rainbow Falls, wildflowers.
CAUTIONS: Trail may be icy in winter. Rocks at falls are slippery.
MAP KEY: 7 C; USGS quad: Mt. Le Conte.
USE: Hiking trail only.
TRAILHEAD: Take Historic Nature Trail—Airport Road (traffic light #8 in Gatlinburg) into the park. At mile 3.4, just after the road becomes one-way, turn right into the Rainbow Falls Parking Area. Find the trail by following a path a few yards south into the woods, opposite the paved road.

The trail goes up the left (east) side of Le Conte Creek. Notice the rocks, from the size of marbles to great boulders. They're on the trail, beside the trail and, especially, in the creek. How would you like to cultivate a garden here? Some did. People lived along the creek and cultivated this rocky land. Before the park was established, these low-lands were logged approximately half way up to Rainbow Falls.

Gatlinburg old-timer Lucinda Ogle remembers when Le Conte Creek was called Mill Creek, because it had so many small gristmills on it. She says there were 14 mills on the main creek and two others

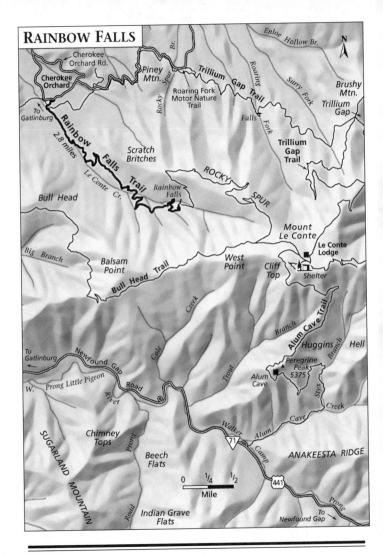

RAINBOW FALLS

N

Enloe Hollow Br.

Cherokee Orchard Rd.

Piney Mtn.

Trillium Gap Trail

Roaring Fork

Surry Fork

Brushy Mtn.

Cherokee Orchard

Roaring Fork Motor Nature Trail

Trillium Gap

To Gatlinburg

Rocky Spur

Rainbow Falls Trail

2.8 miles

Scratch Britches

Falls

Falls Fork

Trillium Gap Trail

Le Conte Cr.

Rainbow Falls

ROCKY

Bull Head

SPUR

Mount Le Conte

Le Conte Lodge

Big Branch

Balsam Point

Bull Head Trail

West Point

Cliff Top

Shelter

Creek

Branch

Alum Cave Trail

Huggins Hell

To Gatlinburg

Newfound Gap

Cole

Trout

Branch

Peregrine Peaks 5375

Alum Cave

Styx

W. Prong Little Pigeon

Road

River

Cave Creek

Chimney Tops

Prong

Walker

Alum

ANAKEESTA RIDGE

Beech Flats

71

Camp

0   1/4   1/2

Mile

441

SUGARLAND MOUNTAIN

Road

Indian Grave Flats

Prong

To Newfound Gap

on small tributaries. The mill she remembers being farthest up the creek was about a quarter-mile upstream from the parking area and about a quarter-mile downstream from the home of Indian Bill. Indian Bill was an herb doctor and the last Cherokee to live in the Gatlinburg area.

The big tree trunk sections decaying on the ground probably are Eastern hemlocks. Look for one of these old logs which is the "nurse" tree for several rosebay rhododendrons growing out of it. Also growing on it is a mat of partridgeberry, the little evergreen ground-hugging vine that produces tiny twin trumpet-shaped flowers and small red berries. The berries are rather tasteless but not unpleasant, something like wet wheat.

After a mile or more, the trail temporarily switches left from the creek and goes through an area where grow rosebay rhododendron, galax, trailing arbutus, teaberry and mountain pepper-bush. Pepper-bush is a shrub that grows a dozen or more feet tall and blooms in mid-summer. Look in this area for pink lady's slippers. You won't find many but you might find one.

The trail switches to the right again and you travel in the general direction of the creek, which you reach and cross on a footbridge about **1.9** miles from where you started walking. In 0.6 mile you'll cross, without help of a bridge, a small tributary of Le Conte Creek.

Then will come the second and third bridges across Le Conte Creek. The third, at **2.7** miles, is just below the falls. If you're here in mid-summer, look for the blooms of pink turtlehead. It's a pretty wildflower that's common at the higher elevations. If you're here in midwinter during a period of prolonged extreme cold, look for the falls to be frozen into an hour-glass shape. This is one of the spectacular sights of the Great Smokies, but it occurs only infrequently.

← *Rainbow Falls*

RICH MOUNTAIN LOOP

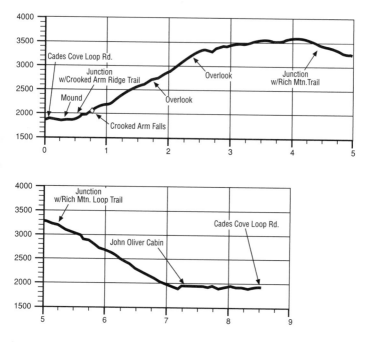

LENGTH: 8.5-mile-long loop hike.
HIGHLIGHTS: Views, wet weather waterfall, John Oliver cabin.
MAP KEY: 3-4 D; USGS quads: Cades Cove, Kinzel Springs.
USE: Horse and hiking trail.
TRAILHEAD: Park at the information shelter near the start of the Cades Cove Loop Road. Walk along the one-way loop road a short distance in the direction of traffic flow. The Rich Mountain Loop Trail begins on the right side of the loop road.

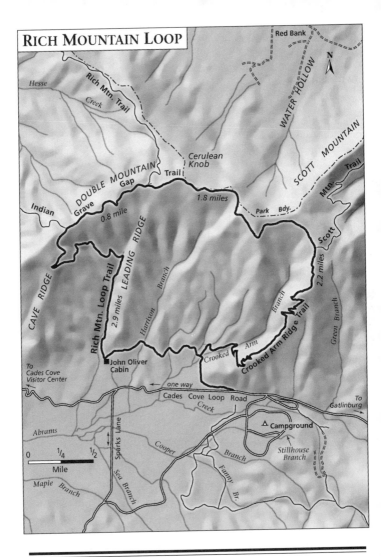

RICH MOUNTAIN LOOP

Red Bank

N

Hesse

Rich Mtn. Trail

WATER HOLLOW

SCOTT MOUNTAIN

Cerulean Knob

Trail

Mtn. Trail

DOUBLE MOUNTAIN

Gap

1.8 miles

Park Bdy.

Scott

Indian

Grave

0.8 mile

LEADING RIDGE

Scott

CAVE RIDGE

Rich Mtn. Loop Trail

2.9 miles

Harrison Branch

Arm Branch

2.2 miles

Green Branch

John Oliver Cabin

Crooked

Crooked Arm Ridge Trail

To Cades Cove Visitor Center

one way

Cades Cove Loop Road

Cove Creek

To Gatlinburg

Abrams

△ Campground

Sparks Lane

Cooper

Branch

Stillhouse Branch

0   ¼   ½

Mile

Jes Branch

Fanny Br.

Maple Branch

This hike is good for spring flowers, fall colors and a broad look at the main range of the Great Smokies. The walk begins and ends within a few yards of the parking area at the beginning of the 11-mile Cades Cove Loop Road.

The first half-mile of your walk is through lowland woods. You'll skirt a meadow to your left, and you might see a deer—or several deer.

You'll cross a small stream, Crooked Arm Branch, and come to a trail fork and a marker which indicates you will reach Rich Mountain by either route. I suggest taking the one to the right, Crooked Arm Ridge Trail, which heads up the creek and then up Crooked Arm Ridge. You'll soon cross back over Crooked Arm Branch and then follow it up to a little waterfall. It's not Niagara, but it's nice.

In spring—say late April or early May—you'll see crested dwarf iris, perhaps flame azalea, blooming locust trees, birdfoot violets, tiny yellow blooms of stargrass and the little cup-like blooms of huckleberry bushes. (Hike here in July and you may find ripe huckleberries.) Occasionally, you will enjoy glimpses of the meadows of Cades Cove and, across the cove, the meandering crest of the Great Smokies' main range.

You also may be puzzled now and then about apparent forks in the trail. Don't be concerned. Take the more obvious route. The others are shortcut routes which hikers and horsemen should never have made. These usually are steep and they erode easily. The last one of these you'll encounter is truly deceptive. One prong leads ahead uphill and slightly to the right, the other downhill and ahead to the left. Take the left fork. (But don't worry if you miss it; you'll soon be back on the right trail, anyway.)

Your next true trail intersection is marked. The trail to the right leads to a campsite and then on to Schoolhouse Gap. Your trail is to the left—to Rich Mountain. You're within 1.5 miles of it.

Your trail soon will become an old Jeep road; good walking. Notice on the bank to your right masses of plants with tough, leathery leaves. Most of these are galax; but the oblong ones are trailing arbutus. The arbutus blooms in March and April, sometimes into May. Blooms are faintly fragrant. Galax sends up a white bloom spike in May and June.

View of Cades Cove along the Rich Mountain loop.

When you find yourself walking the crest of a ridge, look for good views on either side—Cades Cove down to the left and Dry Valley and Tuckaleechee Cove down to the right.

You'll soon reach a point where a trail forks back to your right and up to the top of a knob. This is the peak of Rich Mountain, nearly 1,650 feet higher than where you started walking in the cove. Up here are the foundations of an old fire tower the National Park Service removed several years ago. Because trees ring the small clearing, views are not as good from here as some you've already seen and some you're yet to see. But this is a good place to rest and eat a sandwich.

Back to the old Jeep road and continue in a westerly direction. In October and November, fall-color views up here are magnificent.

Red maples battle scarlet oaks and sourwoods in a war of the reds. Chestnut oaks and black oaks wear less brilliant hues. Sassafras leaves range from lemon to rust. Hickories and tuliptrees wear yellow.

Continue on past the trail that forks to the right that leads to a backcountry campsite and to the park boundary. About 1.5 miles west of the top of Rich Mountain, you'll reach a trail fork. To the right, the road goes to an intersection with the one-way motor road from Cades Cove up over Rich Mountain. Your trail, Rich Mountain Loop Trail, is to the left. It slopes down to your starting point 3.7 miles away.

You'll soon reach a spot where trees have been cleared, leaving you a good view of the main mountain range and Cades Cove. Resume walking. It's mostly downhill the rest of the way. You'll begin crossing tiny streams which join to form Marthas Branch. In the proper season (May, usually) you'll see flame azalea bloom as you skip on down the mountain.

You'll soon be back in the lowland and you will see the small log cabin of John Oliver, one of the earliest settlers of Cades Cove. You also may see deer here, as well as tourists who have left their cars to walk up to the cabin.

Then back to the trail and back to your car.

SILERS BALD—CLINGMANS DOME

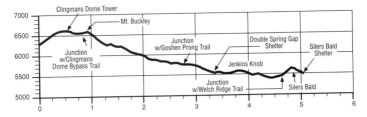

LENGTH: 10 miles roundtrip from Clingmans Dome parking area to Silers Bald and back.
HIGHLIGHTS: Balds, wildflowers.
CAUTIONS: Rocky trail.
MAP KEY: 6-7 E; USGS Quads: Clingmans Dome, Silers Bald.
USE: Hiking trail.
TRAILHEAD: The trail starts from the Clingmans Dome parking area at the end of the Clingmans Dome Road. Start by following the paved trail to the tower.

Nearly all this trail is more than a mile high, and it's an exciting hike you'll long remember.

The first leg is a long half mile, from the Clingmans Dome parking area to Clingmans Dome Tower. At 6,643 feet above sea level, the dome is the highest point in the park and the third highest east of the Mississippi River. The tower gives it an additional 45 feet. From the tower, one can see for miles in every direction on a clear day.

However, I remember a July morning when the sky was not clear. To the contrary, the atmosphere was a sea of mist. It was like trying to look through acres of filmy gauze. The mist was so fine I could not feel it falling. But it collected in droplets on the hairs of my forearms. It collected on the needles of the spruce and fir trees and fell from them in a steady drip, drip, drip. From out of the mist came the Veery's eerie song and the lovely notes of a Winter Wren.

After coming down from the tower, take the narrow trail to the

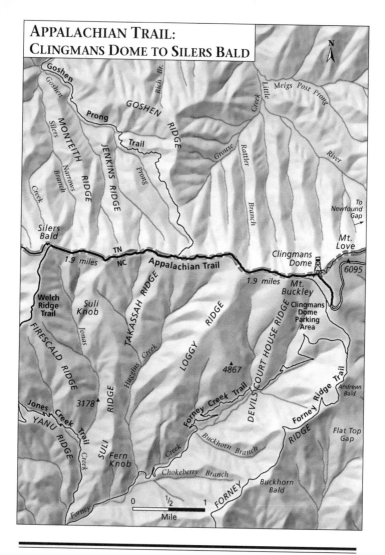

APPALACHIAN TRAIL:
CLINGMANS DOME TO SILERS BALD

N

Goshen

Ridn Br.

GOSHEN RIDGE

Little

Meigs Post Prong

Prong

Goshen

Trail

MONTEITH RIDGE

Silers

JENKINS RIDGE

Prong

Grouse

Rattler

River

Creek

Narrows Branch

Branch

To Newfound Gap

Creek

Silers Bald

Mt. Love

TN

Clingmans Dome

1.9 miles

NC

Appalachian Trail

1.9 miles

6095

Welch Ridge Trail

Suli Knob

TAKASSAH RIDGE

LOGGY RIDGE

Mt. Buckley

Clingmans Dome Parking Area

FIRESCALD RIDGE

Jonas

Higdon Creek

▲4867

DEVILS COURT HOUSE RIDGE

Forney Ridge Trail

Andrews Bald

Jones Creek Trail

3178 ▲

SULI RIDGE

Forney Creek Trail

FORNEY RIDGE

Flat Top Gap

YANU RIDGE

Creek

Fern Knob

Creek

Buckhorn Branch

Chokeberry Branch

FORNEY

Buckhorn Bald

Forney

0   1/2   1
Mile

right and follow it a few feet to the Appalachian Trail. Turn left on it and go westward to Silers Bald.

A quarter of a mile westward is a razorback section of trail barely wide enough to hold the Tennessee-North Carolina boundary. It is followed by a large semi-bald area which is very impressive. This is a world with a different look. Trees on the bald are gnarled and small and few, but grass and weeds grow thickly and about a foot high. There are great patches of thornless blackberries. Late in the season though it was, the blackberries were in full bloom. Blackberries in the lowlands were ripe then.

Also blooming were large purple-fringed orchids (*Platanthera grandiflora*). Though this flower is fairly rare in the Great Smokies, I counted more than 80 on this bald. They're very pretty.

Somewhere down this ragged slope, you may see Turk's cap lilies. Their huge orange-red blooms are dotted with brown. Petals are recurving. Good specimens grow eight feet tall and have up to a dozen blooms. They normally bloom in late July, and I have seen them blooming then, but not on this particular trip, for the season was a late one.

From the bald area, the trail goes back into woodland, composed mostly of spruce and fir but with some American beech and yellow birch. Look for the Double Springs Gap marker. The springs are 50 yards apart. One is 15 yards off the trail on the North Carolina side and the other 35 yards inside Tennessee.

Five or six quail-sized young Ruffed Grouse exploded into the air from near the Tennessee spring when I approached. Their mother quickly followed. (These were the first of more than a dozen grouse I saw on this hike.) A few seconds later, a large hawk sailed through the trees. He probably had had a luncheon interest in the young grouse.

Several yards west of the gap was another fellow who may have had the same interest. This was a red fox. He saw me and raced ahead along the trail and out of sight around a curve. I soon saw him again, still on the trail, and he ran ahead again. I saw him no more till I was on the return trip, and then only once.

Red foxes are indigenous to these highlands, while gray foxes like

the lowlands better. However, some red foxes now are found in the lowlands because fox hunters have imported them and turned them loose there.

Another highland animal you may see is the little red squirrel called the "boomer." You won't find him in the lowlands of East Tennessee, but you would find him, or some of his close kin, in similar spruce-fir forests of Canada and New England.

A low-growing flower you'll see under thick stands of spruce and fir is wood-sorrel (*Oxalis montana*), which looks like a shamrock. It has three leaves and a small white bloom threaded with pink. It can thrive under the spruce and fir because it requires very little sunlight.

The first bald you reach west of Double Springs Gap is a small one, decorated with a few flame azalea and laurel bushes. But this is not Silers. You have more walking to do.

Not far beyond the small bald is the Narrows, a rocky section where the mountain crest is little wider than the trail. This is the only part of the hike where the altitude dips a little below 5,500'.

The trail forks at the foot of Silers. The left fork angles down Welch Ridge and the right one climbs Silers. The climb to the top of Silers is steep but mercifully short.

Silers is a large bald, mostly grassy but with some blackberries and a few heath plants. The elevation at the top is 5,607 feet. Go down the western slope to the Appalachian Trailer shelter. A good spring is near.

Take a good rest. The way back is long and often steep.

Return by the same route, except for the last half mile. At the trail junction, take the bypass trail to Clingmans Dome Parking Area, rather than the left one to the dome. Turn left at the next trail intersection, and follow the trail through an area of tremendous boulders to the parking area.

(If you want a short loop hike of less than two miles, rather than the long one to Silers, do only the first and last legs of the long hike. Go to the tower, get on the Appalachian Trail and follow it down to the first marked intersection. Turn sharply left onto the bypass trail. Turn left again at the next intersection and go back to your car.)

← *Observation tower atop Clingmans Dome, 6,643 feet.*

SMOKEMONT LOOP

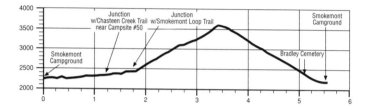

LENGTH: 6.1-mile-long loop hike, including 0.5 mile through the campground (not shown on elevation profile).
HIGHLIGHTS: Pretty streams, wildflowers.
MAP KEY: 8 E; USGS quad: Smokemont.
USE: Horse and hiking trail.
TRAILHEAD: Start this hike in D Loop of Smokemont Campground. Take Bradley Fork Trail 1.7 miles to Smokemont Loop Trail, which, as the name implies, will loop back to the campground. There is some parking at the trailhead, more at the hiker parking area near the campground entrance.

The way to do this pleasant loop hike is start on Bradley Fork Trail and finish on Smokemont Loop. Bradley Fork Trail is an old road along the Bradley Fork of the Oconaluftee River. The lower part is used heavily by horses from Smokemont Riding Stable, but it is firm and well-graded, with a bridge at every creek crossing.

The trail starts with Bradley Fork on the left and a high bank with dog-hobble and rosebay rhododendron on the right. As the trail rises, a connector from the horse stable merges from the right. Some hikers and perhaps some horses have made destructive shortcuts between the two trails.

The trail drops back to creek level with a mossy bench on the left and a spur trail to the water. After a brown cinder block pump house on the right, a utility road forks right, and Bradley Fork Trail continues straight into a forest of small trees and lush ferns and mosses. It

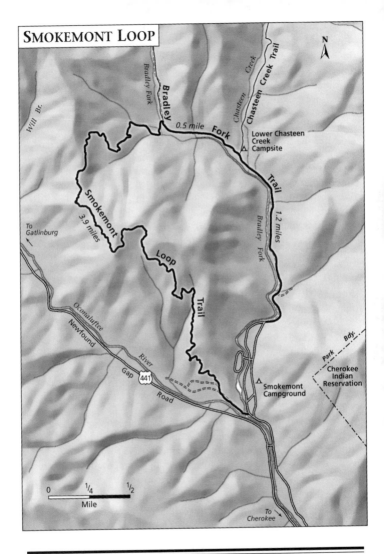

SMOKEMONT LOOP

N

Will Br.

Bradley Fork

Bradley Fork

Chasteen Creek

Chasteen Creek Trail

0.5 mile

Lower Chasteen
Creek
Campsite

Smokemont
3.9 miles

Trail

Bradley Fork

1.2 miles

To Gatlinburg

Loop

Oconaluftee

Newfound

River

Gap

441

Road

Park Bdy.

Cherokee
Indian
Reservation

Smokemont
Campground

0   ¼   ½
Mile

To
Cherokee

alternates between open areas with tall weeds and thin forest of flowering dogwood, yellow birch, sycamore, and tuliptree. At **1.1** mile, the trail crosses a side creek on a wooden bridge and then reaches the junction with Chasteen Creek Trail at **1.2** miles. From here it is just 0.1 mile to Campsite #50, one of the easiest backcountry campsites to reach, and 4.0 miles up to Hughes Ridge. Chasteen Falls is 0.7 mile up Chasteen Creek Trail, a nice side trip if you've got the time and energy.

After the trail sign, notice a creek overflow channel on the left. This is one of the many signs that Bradley Fork sometimes carries a lot of water. It drains a large, U-shaped basin framed by Richland Mountain, 6 miles of the Smokies crest, and Hughes Ridge. The trail rises a bit, with a sand bank on the right, and then enters thin woods. About 0.5 mile farther, it reaches a bench and the Smokemont Loop Trail. After your sit, take the Smokemont Loop Trail.

The loop trail begins by crossing Bradley Fork on a long, skinny foot log. This is one of the longest foot logs I have ever used in the Smokies, and it is a bouncy, narrow experience. You'll be grateful for the hand rail. Across the fork, the trail immediately heads south for about 100 yards before turning sharply right and uphill. An unmarked trail continues along the water, but it is not the true path.

You climb steadily through a mixed hardwood forest. The area is rather wet and supports lots of spring and summer wildflowers like crested dwarf iris, spotted wintergreen, and Indian pipe. Both spring and fall are pleasant seasons for this route—the former offering wildflower color, the latter featuring a mix of fall color from maples, flowering dogwoods, and tuliptrees. A summer hike might be muddy and buggy, though still pretty.

The trail soon veers away from the fork and into a higher, drier forest. While most of the trees are young, occasional giant tuliptrees allow for a more open understory. After about **2.5** miles, pine trees, hickories, grasses, and briers signal a dry slope and provide some good views to the east and northeast before the trail switches back to the west side of the ridge.

At this point, you're likely to hear auto noise from Newfound Gap Road. The slope steepens here too, and you embark on a long uphill pull of about 1.0 mile, bringing you finally to a knob at the top of the ridge **3.4** miles along. Next comes a 180 degree switchback that turns back east toward Chasteen Creek and, mercifully, downhill. This side of the ridge features more and older hardwoods. Within a quarter mile the trail passes through a distinct saddle between two ridges that would make a nice picnic spot. It is gently sloped and grassy under a grove of big, mixed hardwoods.

The trail winds its way down the ridge uneventfully until about a half mile from the campground. Growing under a canopy of mixed oaks and pines, sweet peas, wild roses, and sawbriers signal the site of a homestead. More evidence of former habitation appears a few hundred feet ahead when you encounter an old cemetery down the slope. People have climbed down to the graveyard at numerous spots, creating steep and eroded side trails, but better access is provided a few hundred yards further along via a maintained spur trail at mile **5.4**.

This cemetery is commonly known as the Bradley Cemetery, named for a family that settled in the region during the beginning of the nineteenth century. It contains 30-50 graves that date from the late 1800s to 1925. Some are weathered to the point that no inscription can be read. Those that are still legible have Bradley, Wilson, and Reagan family names.

Bradleytown was the name for the Smokemont region before the establishment of organized logging activities in the early 1900s. Smokemont acquired its current name when a town grew up around a saw mill used by Champion Fibre Company.

Smokemont Campground is only a short walk beyond the cemetery. The trail joins with a service road and crosses a bridge into the campground 0.5 mile from the Bradley Fork trailhead (D Loop) to your left.

STRENUOUS HIKES

ALUM CAVE BLUFF & MT. LE CONTE

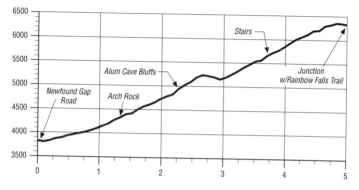

LENGTH: 4.5 miles roundtrip from Newfound Gap Road to the bluffs and back; 10 miles roundtrip from Newfound Gap Road to the summit of Mt. Le Conte and back.

HIGHLIGHTS: Arch Rock, Alum Cave Bluffs, old-growth forest, views, Inspiration Point, Mt. Le Conte.

CAUTIONS: Ice on trail, icicles falling from bluffs in winter. This is one of the most heavily-traveled trails in the park.

MAP KEY: 7 D; USGS quad: Mt. Le Conte.

USE: Hiking trail.

TRAILHEAD: Drive 8.6 miles on Newfound Gap Road (U.S. 441) from Sugarlands Visitor Center (or 20 miles from Oconaluftee Visitor Center). There is a sign and two large parking areas marking the trailhead.

This very popular hike is good at any season, but it is prettiest in early June, the normal time for Catawba rhododendron to bloom. The well-maintained trail leaves the Newfound Gap Road at the Alum Cave Bluffs parking area and crosses and recrosses Alum Cave Creek for the first 1.3 miles.

This little stream is unusually pretty, even for the Great Smokies. But it can become huge and destructive after flooding summer storms

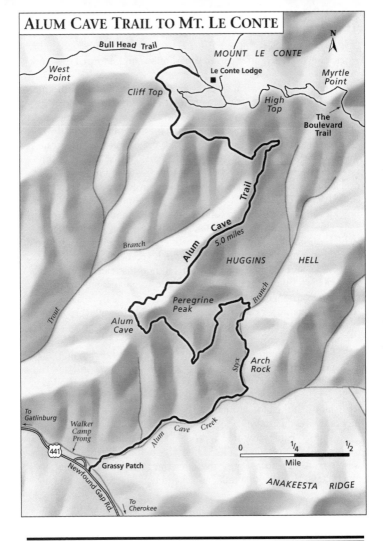

ALUM CAVE TRAIL TO MT. LE CONTE

N

Bull Head Trail

MOUNT LE CONTE

West Point

Le Conte Lodge

Myrtle Point

Cliff Top

High Top

The Boulevard Trail

Branch

Alum Cave Trail

5.0 miles

HUGGINS HELL

Branch

Peregrine Peak

Trout

Alum Cave

Styx

Arch Rock

To Gatlinburg

Walker Camp Prong

441

Newfound Gap Rd.

Alum Cave Creek

Grassy Patch

0   1/4   1/2
Mile

To Cherokee

ANAKEESTA RIDGE

---

strike in the mountains it drains. As you walk along this trail, look for the debris still visible from such a storm that poured down a great volume of water on September 1, 1951. The trunks of great trees still lie where they were left after this stream subsided and returned to its normal course.

The same 1951 storm caused earthslides high on the southern slopes of Mt. Le Conte, part of which is drained by this stream.

Subsequent storms in the 1970s and 1993 caused landslides and massive erosion gulleys that uncovered a kind of rock called the Anakeesta formation. It's an acid-bearing stone, and after the stone was uncovered the acid leached into the creek, either killing or driving out the Appalachian brook trout that then lived in it. Time probably will heal the wound to the mountainside and the trout can come back to the stream, where I once caught and released a 10-inch brookie. (It now is illegal to fish for brook trout in most park streams.)

The trail winds through thick growth of rosebay rhododendron (which normally blooms in late June or early July) before reaching a fine forest composed mostly of yellow birch and hemlock.

Creek and trail stay close together a short distance beyond Arch Rock. This formation is what you'd expect—a great stone arch. The trail climbs through it on a flight of stone steps. The rock is black slate. The opening, now large enough for people to walk through with ease, started as a crack thousands of years ago. Weathering and frost action caused its growth.

The next important point of interest is a large heath bald through which the trail passes. Growing here are laurel, sand myrtle, a few blueberry bushes and a great deal of rose-pink Catawba rhododendron. It's the rhododendron that makes the splashy show. If the season is normal, the bloom is best June 5-15. It blooms a few days later higher up the mountain.

A heath bald sometimes is called a laurel slick, and mountaineers used to call them "laurel hells." They were hell to get through if there was no trail. The bushes grow in such a tight tangle that nothing much larger than a chipmunk can get through a laurel hell without cussing.

Not far beyond the heath bald, you get your first look at Alum

Cave Bluffs. It's all bluff, not a cave. But what a bluff! This overhanging mountain of black slate could shelter hundreds. It is nearly 100 yards long, with an overhang of 20 to 25 yards at its widest point. A marker that once stood here said:

"This high overhanging cliff is the result of weathering of black slate at its base. This slate contains an abundance of iron sulfide; weak sulfuric acid formed by the weathering of the sulfide has decomposed the slate, resulting in the dust which covers the ground."

"Ground waters seeping through the rock have picked up a certain amount of mineral matter and deposited it on the face of the bluff in the form of alum. It is only a thin film and not of commercial importance. Nevertheless, a persistent legend has it that saltpeter was found here in considerable quantities during the Civil War and that it was converted into gunpowder."

The gunpowder legend apparently is without basis. What was manufactured here, from near 1840 at least into the 1890s, was Epsom salts. It was not a large operation, just one or two cabins for workers and some vats for boiling the cliff crumblings. One operator, the Epsom Salts Manufacturing Co., was sold for taxes.

Leaving the bluffs, the trail passes an excellent view down the rocky spine of Little Duck Hawk Ridge. Climbing steeply, the trail swings around the ridge at a small side trail that leads several yards to Gracies Pulpit. This rocky promontory is named for Gracie McNichol, an early matron of Mt. Le Conte who is noted for climbing the mountain many, many times, including on her 92nd birthday. From the rocks there is a fine view of the Le Conte massif, rising above the valley of Trout Branch. You can see the four peaks comprising the massif: West Point, Cliff Top, High Top, and Myrtle Point.

The trail descends 80' during the next 0.4 mile as it travels across an unnamed saddle, then climbs in earnest to the summit of Mt. Le Conte. The trail enters a grove of particularly healthy virgin red spruce in a distinctive uplands forest. Soon you will pass a slide (now overgrown with briars, yellow birch saplings, and American mountain ash) where a switchback in the trail was washed away during heavy rains in the 1970s and again during December 1992. The trail was re-routed by installing the present stairs at mile **3.8**.

Alum Cave Bluffs

In its last mile the trail alternates between grassy scars of landslides and red spruce forest. Above 6,000', dead Fraser fir dominate what once was a beautiful forest. A combination of the balsam woolly adelgid, which has infested the Fraser fir, and acid precipitation, which has sickened the red spruce, has almost removed the "sprucefir" designation from the southern Appalachians. The forest now consists of red spruce, mountain ash, and an understory of hobblebush, briars, and mosses.

Leaving the forest, the trail traverses the steep rock face below Cliff Top. This area receives little sunlight during the winter, and the trail is often covered with ice. The steel cables provide handholds in any weather, but especially in winter. Once the climb is over, you'll arrive at the saddle between Cliff Top and West Point.

The trail swings around the mountain top, with views of Gatlinburg and Pigeon Forge; on exceptionally clear days you can even see downtown Knoxville, TN. Young Fraser fir grow all around you. Look for wildflowers such as bluebead lily, pink turtlehead, and filmy angelica. The trail ends at a junction with Rainbow Falls Trail, a few hundred yards from Le Conte Lodge.

Two of Le Conte's three peaks—Myrtle Point and Cliff Top— offer thrilling views of mountain wilderness. Each has a "specialty." Myrtle Point is for sunrises and Cliff Top is for sunsets.

However, unless you want to hike in darkness, seeing sunrise and sunset from these points requires spending the night on Le Conte. Le Conte Lodge can house some 50 overnight guests. A shelter similar to those on the Appalachian Trail accommodates a dozen. Those intending to stay in the shelter must obtain a permit, and, of course, they should bring food. There is a reasonable charge for staying at the lodge, which also provides supper and breakfast for overnight guests.

At 6,593 feet above sea level, Mt. Le Conte is the third highest peak in the park, 50 feet lower than Clingmans Dome and 28 feet lower than Mt. Guyot. However, some Le Conte fans scorn this formula of comparison. They say Le Conte is the "tallest" peak east of the Rocky Mountains. They mean that it towers higher above its immediate base than does any other peak. The base, at Gatlinburg, is 1,292 feet above sea level. That makes Le Conte a mile and 21 feet "tall."

Le Conte Lodge is the highest resort east of the Mississippi River. Situated on a clearing in a forest of spruce and fir, it looks like a frontier outpost. Seven or eight balsam log cabins are guest sleeping quarters. Two large ones are three-bedroom buildings, with the bedrooms built in a half circle around a large livingroom. Each bedroom has a double-decker bed that sleeps four. It is always cool on Le Conte. The mercury has never been known to top 80°F there.

A large shingled building houses the dining room and kitchen and the living quarters for the operators.

The first man to operate a guest facility atop Le Conte was Paul Adams. Under contract with Great Smoky Mountains Conservation Association (which was backing establishment of a national park in the Great Smokies), Paul began operations in 1925. His first guests slept in a large tent. He later built a cabin. He started operations near the same spring that provides water for the present Le Conte Lodge. This spring is believed to be the highest constant-flow spring in eastern North America. It is a few feet more than 6,300 feet above sea level.

Jack Huff took over from Paul in 1926 and started developing the Lodge that is there today. Huff climbed Le Conte hundreds of times. One thing troubled him: His aging mother had never seen the world from Le Conte's lofty peaks. A semi-invalid, she was not able to hike or ride a horse.

So Jack fashioned a special chair which he could strap onto his back. And that's how he carried his 90-pound mother to Mt. Le Conte. He said she was the only person who ever went to Le Conte backwards.

Jack and his wife, Pauline, were married at sunrise on Myrtle Point April 1934. They operated the Lodge through the 1949 season, after which Jack had to operate the family-owned Mountain View Hotel because of his father's death. Pauline continued to operate the Lodge through the 1959 season. The Huffs then sold their interests to another couple who loved the mountains, Herrick and Myrtle Brown.

The Browns took over the Lodge in 1960 under a lease arrangement with the National Park Service. Myrtle soon learned that cooking on Le Conte involves special problems. It takes 50 minutes to boil potatoes on Le Conte, compared with 20 minutes in Gatlinburg. Pauline years earlier had worked out a special recipe for Le Conte pancakes. The high altitude, with its lower boiling point, causes the problem.

Cliff Top and Myrtle Point are rocky, nature-made platforms, with views of hundreds of square miles of mountains and distant lowlands. The lights of Knoxville and smaller East Tennessee towns are visible on clear nights.

Though virtually treeless, Cliff Top and Myrtle Point have thick patches of the small Carolina rhododendron and the shorter sand myrtle. Sand myrtle is a little evergreen with glossy leaves not much larger than a mouse's ear and pretty pink-white blooms. It usually blooms in the first half of June at this altitude, while the Carolina rhododendron blooms a little later.

Myrtle Point is nearly a mile from the Lodge. It is reached by crossing High Top, Le Conte's highest point. Though a little higher than Cliff Top and Myrtle Point, High Top offers no good view because it is covered with trees. Cliff Top is about a quarter of a mile from the Lodge.

A good early-morning routine, particularly for a bird watcher, is to get out of bed in time to reach Myrtle Point for the sunrise scene.

Make the return slowly. Breakfast isn't nearly ready. Take a side hike a quarter of a mile out the Boulevard Trail. You'll hear the haunting song of the Veery and the long, lovely song of the Winter Wren. Only a careful birder can get a look at the shy Veery, but you can see the stub-tailed wren sitting on the tip top of a tree. Other birds you may see include American Robins, Dark-eyed Juncos, Red-breasted Nuthatches, Golden-crowned Kinglets, Solitary Vireos, and Chestnut-sided, Black-throated Blue, Canada and Blackburnian Warblers. The warblers, the veery and the vireo are only summer residents at this altitude.

Five major trails lead to Le Conte. For hikers who have two cars, or who can otherwise arrange transportation, I suggest going by way of the Alum Cave Trail and returning by way of the Boulevard Trail and the Appalachian Trail, about 13 miles total. The latter follows the high Boulevard Ridge 5.4 miles southward from Le Conte to the main crest of the Great Smokies. Turn west there on the Appalachian Trail and follow it 2.7 miles to where a car better be waiting at Newfound Gap. From the crest of Boulevard Ridge, one can see some of the most rugged regions of the Great Smokies.

Those who have only one car but who want to ascend and descend by different trails can leave from Cherokee Orchard and take the Rainbow Falls Trail, 6.5 miles, and return on the Bullhead Trail, 6.8 miles. The Bullhead offers magnificent autumn scenery. Interesting features of the Rainbow Falls Trail are the falls, where Le

Conte Creek takes a mighty leap, and Rocky Spur, good for rose-pink rhododendron. The Bullhead heath bald is fine for spring blooms and contrasting fall colors on the Bullhead Trail.

The Lodge has become so popular that reserving a weekend there usually has to be done during the year before you want to go. A week-night reservation is a little easier to get. Those who can't get Lodge reservations at the time they want them can try with the park service for reservations at the shelter. A good hiker can solve the problem by making the round-trip hike all in the same day, but he misses the sunset and sunrise sessions at Cliff Top and Myrtle Point.

Ages of those who have hiked to Le Conte range from less than four to more than 90. The Browns' daughter Barbara hiked all the way up the Alum Cave Trail when she was three and a half years old.

Employees at Le Conte Lodge commonly use Alum Cave Trail as their route to and from work, and they become proficient hikers over the season. The current record for leaving the lodge, descending Alum Cave Trail, driving to Gatlinburg, purchasing beer, then returning is 2 hours and 50 minutes. Another Le Conte employee, on an emergency quest for popcorn and a newspaper, descended the trail in 33 minutes, then completed the return trip in only 1 hour and 18 minutes. The park service, however, considers the Alum Cave Trail round trip to Mt. Le Conte a six to eight hour excursion, so you should devote a whole day to the hike, unless you're staying at the lodge or shelter.

CHIMNEY TOPS TRAIL

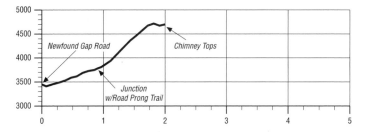

LENGTH: 4.0 miles roundtrip, from Newfound Gap Road to the Chimney Tops and back.

HIGHLIGHTS: View from the top, big trees.

CAUTIONS: Steep trail, ice in winter, pinnacles at the top.

MAP KEY: 7 D; USGS quad: Mt. Le Conte.

USE: Hiking trail.

TRAILHEAD: Drive 6.7 miles south from Sugarlands Visitor Center on Newfound Gap Road (or 22 miles north from Oconaluftee Visitor Center). Look for a large parking area on the west side of the road between the lower tunnel and "the loop."

The Chimney Tops Trail is one of the most popular in the park because of its length and spectacular view, but it is a steady uphill hike and could be hazardous at the top. If you are hiking with children, establish some safety rules before starting out. The rock outcrops at the top are steep, slippery when wet or icy, and exposed to wind and lightning. If there are several buses in the parking lot, you might want to choose another hike and do the Chimneys later.

This watershed was not as heavily logged as the Little River drainage just to the west over Sugarland Mountain, because of extensive private ownership and because land controlled by Champion Fibre Company was condemned for park purchase just in time to save its old-growth forest. Mary Brackin was born just below the Chimney Tops in 1889 and married Marshall Whaley at age 16. Throughout

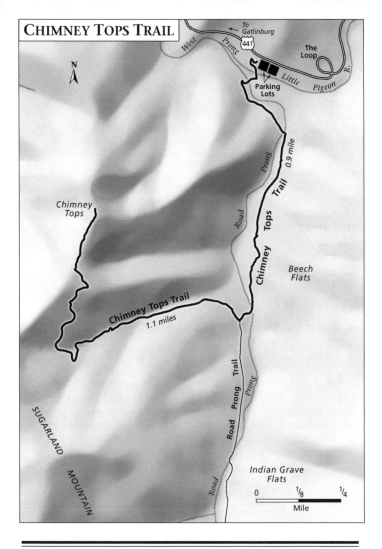

CHIMNEY TOPS TRAIL

To Gatlinburg

441

The Loop

West Prong

Little Pigeon R.

Parking Lots

N

Prong

0.9 mile

Chimney Tops Trail

Chimney Tops

Beech Flats

Road

Chimney Tops Trail

1.1 miles

Road Prong Trail

Prong

SUGARLAND

MOUNTAIN

Road

Indian Grave Flats

0   1/8   1/4

Mile

their marriage, she "put as much meat on the table as he did. I'd go up one hollow with a rifle and he'd go up another, and I'd come back with as many squirrels as he would."

From the parking area, hike down through Eastern hemlocks and listen as water noise replaces traffic. At the first bridge, across Walker Camp Prong of Little Pigeon River, you see huge smooth boulders and a deep green pool downstream. At the other end of the bridge, on the right, is a Fraser magnolia with eight trunks. Look for its large lobed leaves. These deciduous magnolias, common up to 5,000', produce creamy white, pie-sized flowers in late April or early May and live only in the southern Appalachians.

The trail rises and crosses Road Prong, which joins Walker Camp Prong to form West Prong of the Little Pigeon River. The bridges are new and sturdy with three rails. Many spring wildflowers grow along the side, including trillium and hepatica. Later in summer, you will see bee-balm, jewelweed and Joe-Pye-weed. After the fourth bridge, about **0.9** mile from the trailhead, you pass the junction with the Road Prong Trail. Continuing right, the Chimney Tops Trail leaves the Road Prong behind, and, after a switchback, starts up a small creek valley. As the trail steepens, the rhododendron gives way to a mixed forest. Toothworts, foamflowers, and violets grow in the mossy bank. The valley becomes a ravine, with high ridges sheltering it.

Here you meet the stars and giants of this trail: yellow buckeye trees, the only palmately compound tree in the park—that is, each leaf has five leaflets extending from the leaf stalk like outstretched fingers. Look for a tree with those leaves, twigs that sit opposite each other on the branch, and bark with ripple patterns where the outer layer has peeled off. Because buckeyes grow in sheltered coves, and their seeds cannot germinate if they dry out, their presence indicates that this area was not farmed or logged extensively. Young buckeyes sometimes jump the gun and put out leaves in March, only to lose them in the next frost. But they have spare buds and can try again later. The flowers appear in May and look like a formal yellow-and-white corsage. In the big cluster of flowers, only one or two produce nuts, which fall in September. The nuts contain a poisonous narcotic alkaloid, and farmers moved their cattle away from buckeye coves in the fall. Indians made the nuts edible by roasting, grinding, and leaching out the poison. Squirrels either discard the poisonous part or are not affected by it.

Carrying a buckeye nut is said to give good luck, as long as you don't chew on it. Look for round, leathery capsules on the trail and break them open to reveal shiny mahogany brown nuts with a wood grain pattern. The nut will shrivel unless oiled. If you don't have any mink oil along, human oil will do: rub the buckeye along the side of your nose to bring out the rich mahogany color.

After a metal culvert, the trail becomes steep and rocky. The creek ripples down a mossy cascade on the right. Another creek comes in from the left, and after another metal culvert, the trail turns left to ascend a steep slope to a switchback. Please don't cut across this switchback—unauthorized trails cause erosion and habitat destruction. After the switchback, the trail ascends easily along Sugarland Mountain. Toward the top of the next ridge tall spruces branch over the valley. Next to a dead spruce is an opening with a view of Mount Le Conte. The trail descends and then levels along the top of a narrow ridge.

Facing you is a ridged, sloping rock pinnacle. A sign warns hikers not to venture beyond the two peaks of the Chimney Tops and reminds them how much rescue efforts cost. Some people scramble up the rock face, but there is an alternate path to the right with access to the top of the rock. However, even this route has risky parts. Rocky handholds have been polished by sweaty hands until they shine like antique banisters. And these rocks qualify as antiques. They are part of the Anakeesta Formation, which is exposed in outcrops like this and Charlies Bunion. Anakeesta metamorphic slate is at least 600 million years old, laid down during the Pre-Cambrian Era.

From the top you can see another rocky hump farther along. Some hikers try to continue out to this second hump, although it is extremely dangerous to do so. Many injuries have occurred out there. The chimney holes are to the left of the rocks and should be viewed with extreme caution. The main shaft is big enough to fall into. Look back down onto Newfound Gap Road and across the valley to Mount Le Conte; the steep side of Sugarland Mountain appears opposite.

Chimney Tops →

GREGORY BALD

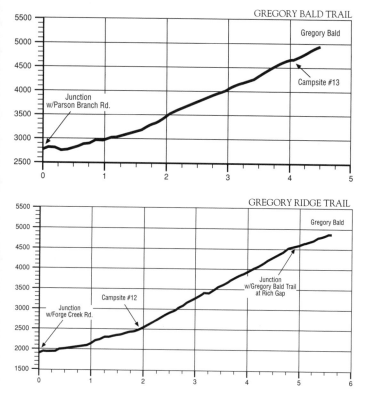

LENGTH: 9.0 miles roundtrip on Gregory Bald Trail; 11.4 miles roundtrip on Gregory Ridge Trail; 14.2 miles roundtrip via Gregory Ridge Trail, Gregory Bald Trail, and Parson Branch Road (walking on road).

HIGHLIGHTS: Flame azaleas in late June, views from bald, old-growth forest on Gregory Ridge Trail.

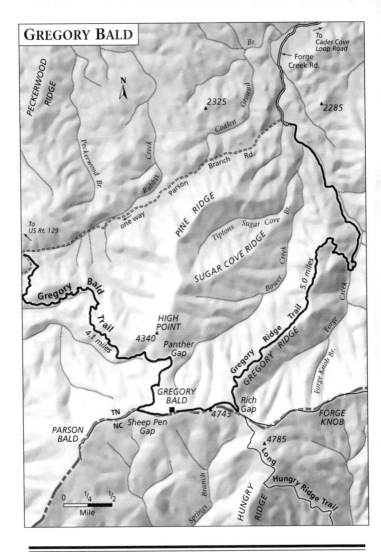

GREGORY BALD

PECKERWOOD RIDGE

N

2325

Goalen Ground

2285

To Cades Cove Loop Road

Forge Creek Rd.

Peckerwood Br.

Rabbit Creek

Parson Branch Rd.

one way

To US Rt. 129

PINE RIDGE

Tiptons Sugar Cove

Sugar Cove Br.

SUGAR COVE RIDGE

Bower Creek

Gregory Bald

Trail

4.1 miles

HIGH POINT
▲4340

Panther Gap

5.0 miles

Gregory Ridge Trail

GREGORY RIDGE

Forge Knob Br.

Forge Creek

GREGORY BALD

■

4743

Rich Gap

FORGE KNOB

TN

NC

Sheep Pen Gap

PARSON BALD

▲4785

Long

HUNGRY RIDGE

Hungry Ridge Trail

Springs Branch

0   ¼   ½

Mile

MAP KEY: F-2; USGS quads: Calderwood, Cades Cove.
USE: Gregory Ridge Trail is hiking only, Gregory Bald Trail is horse and hiking.
TRAILHEAD: Gregory Ridge Trail starts at the end of Forge Creek Road, which begins just past Cades Cove Visitor Center on the Cades Cove Loop Road. Gregory Bald Trail starts from Sams Gap on one-way Parson Branch Road (closed in winter) which also originates from Forge Creek Road.

If you can hike only once to Gregory Bald, go when the flame azaleas bloom. Best time usually is June 15-25. Before you do, though, check with park officials to learn whether the bloom is on schedule.

The "most gay and brilliant flowering shrub yet known" was William Bartram's description of flame azaleas. Bartram, first botanist to visit the Southern Appalachians, had his first look at flame azaleas in 1776.

Go to Gregory and you probably will agree with him. Hundreds, probably thousands, of azaleas bloom there. They are white, pink, yellow, orange and a striking orange-red. Most numerous are the orange and yellow.

Gregory is the second or third largest of several balds in the Great Smokies. There are two types—grass balds and heath balds. Gregory is classed as a grass bald because grass is its predominant cover. A heath bald is one thickly covered with heath plants—mostly laurel and rhododendron.

How the grass balds came to be is a mystery. Fire and grazing have been advanced as possible reasons why the forest which covers the surrounding area does not also cover them. Indians said the gods cleared them.

Dr. Randolph Shields, a botanist who was born and reared in Cades Cove, below Gregory, says the bald area has dwindled considerably since he herded sheep and cattle there in his youth. Back then, the cove dwellers summered their herds on Gregory and two other large grass balds, Spence Field and Russell Field. Livestock fattened well on the lush wild grass.

The forest has crept upward year by year since the land became part of the park and grazing was stopped, in the early 1930s. This place of grass and flowers now contains only about fifteen acres. Shields says it was several times that large when he herded on it.

But the National Park Service now is trying to reverse Gregory's trend to forest. It is cutting back forest growth and it also is cutting out some of the heath shrubs. The objective is to maintain the bald similar to what it was in the 1940s—mostly grass but with a scattering of azaleas.

The National Park Service also is trying to protect some sensitive areas in the bald vicinity from the rooting of European wild hogs. You may see fences which keep the wild hogs out of some fragile wildflower areas.

Azaleas grow thickest in a fringe around the edge of the bald, where the grass and forest meet. However, they are scattered all over, along with a few blueberry and serviceberry bushes. Most of these azaleas are thickly branched, sturdy and rather squat, compared with slender, taller ones that grow in the woods along the trails to Gregory. Gregory is 4,949 feet above sea level at its highest point, but the bald area extends down to about the 4,800-foot contour line.

If you are thirsty and have no water, try an azalea gall. They are greenish-white, about the size of a baby's hand, and they grow on azalea branches. Most persons aren't really fond of them; however, some are. They have little taste, but what they do have reminds one faintly of that part of a watermelon where the red fades into the white-green rind. They're full of liquid.

What is the best route to get to Gregory? Two trails lead there from the Cades Cove area. The Forge Creek Road breaks off the Cades Cove loop road, only a few feet beyond the entrance to the Cable Mill historic area. Follow it to where it dead ends at a turn-around. The Gregory Ridge Trail starts at the turn-around.

The other trail is the Gregory Bald Trail. Reach it by following Forge Creek Road also, but turn right off it onto the Parson Branch Road and follow the latter four miles to the Gregory Bald Trail at Sams Gap.

A word of caution: In your planning, remember the Parson Branch Road is one-way. The gates at both ends are closed at night. If

you intend to make a loop hike—going by one trail and returning by the other, you may as well plan to walk the Parson Branch Road, leaving your car outside the gate. The alternative is to have a friend pick you up at the end of the hike.

If you walk the road and make the loop hike, your round trip is about 14.2 miles. If you ascend and descend the Gregory Bald Trail, leaving your car on the Parson Branch Road, your round trip is about 9 miles. If you go and return by the Gregory Ridge Trail, the round trip is 11.4 miles. If you go by Gregory Ridge and return by Gregory Bald Trail, having someone to meet you at the end of the trail, your round trip is about 10.2 miles.

If you ascend and descend by the same route, I suggest the Gregory Ridge Trail. This is because you should not miss the exceptional beauty of the first mile or two of this trail, in Forge Creek Valley. Magnificent hemlock and tulip trees grow here.

I recall going up one of the trails and coming back the other with Arthur Stupka and his first wife, Margaret, and Shields. Stupka, park naturalist for many years and later park biologist, was an authority on everything that blooms, walks, crawls, flies and sings in the mountains. He was particularly good on birds.

And he was working birds this misty morning on the Gregory Bald Trail. He listened for their songs, often checking the altimeter he carried and making notes on the altitudes at which he first heard various species. We listened to simultaneous serenades from a Scarlet Tanager and a Rose-breasted Grosbeak. We saw three or four of each. The Scarlet Tanager is to birddom in the Eastern United States what Bartram said of flame azaleas—the "most gay and brilliant."

We startled a Dark-eyed Junco which had a nest on the ground in a thick patch of wood betony beside the trail. She left in such a hurry that she kicked one of her four mottled eggs from her nest. Margaret found the nest and put back the egg.

← *Flame azalea shrubs on Gregory Bald.*

GROTTO FALLS & BRUSHY MOUNTAIN

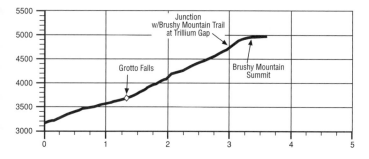

LENGTH: From Roaring Fork Motor Nature Trail: 2.6 miles roundtrip to Grotto Falls and back; 7.2 miles roundtrip to the top of Brushy Mountain and back.

HIGHLIGHTS: Grotto Falls, views, diversity of plant life.

CAUTIONS: Some difficult creek crossings in rainy weather..

MAP KEY: 7 C-D; USGS quad: Le Conte.

USE: Horse, llama (for Le Conte Lodge), and hiking trail.

TRAILHEAD: Take Historic Nature Trail—Airport Road (traffic light #8) from the main street in Gatlinburg (U.S. 441). Drive to the park boundary, past the Twin Creeks Road and Ogle home site, and into Cherokee Orchard. Continue on to Roaring Fork Motor Nature Trail (closed in winter) and follow it to the large parking area for the Trillium Gap Trail to Grotto Falls.

This part of the Trillium Gap Trail starts in a pretty Eastern hemlock grove with many large, old-growth trees. Big American beeches, silverbells, and maples share space with the hemlocks in this mature forest, and you can find rotting trunks that support little trees and shrubs. You might also see more recently dead snags and stumps that have been worked over by Pileated Woodpeckers. If fresh splinters of wood have been scattered on the ground and if there are rectangular holes big and deep enough to stick your hand into, this woodpecker—

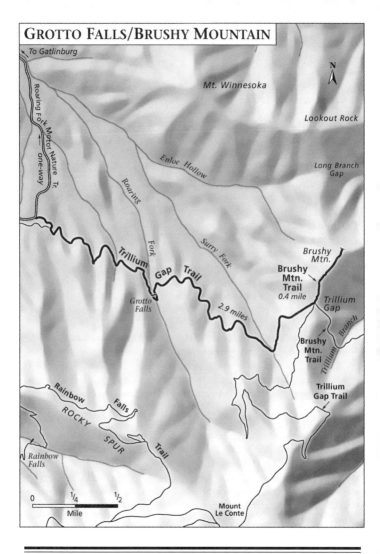

GROTTO FALLS/BRUSHY MOUNTAIN

To Gatlinburg

Roaring Fork Motor Nature Tr.

one-way

N

Mt. Winnesoka

Lookout Rock

Enloe Hollow

Long Branch Gap

Roaring

Fork

Surry Fork

Brushy Mtn.

Trillium Gap Trail

Grotto Falls

2.9 miles

Brushy Mtn. Trail 0.4 mile

Trillium Gap

Brushy Mtn. Trail

Trillium Branch

Trillium Gap Trail

Rainbow Falls

ROCKY SPUR Trail

Rainbow Falls

0   ¼   ½

Mile

Mount Le Conte

the largest of the region—has probably been there. You might hear its crazy laughing call or glimpse a flash of a black and white crow-sized bird flying from trunk to trunk. It doesn't bother healthy trees, just dead or dying ones.

The trail rises steadily, following a typical Smokies hiking pattern: in toward a creek, cross, out around a ridge, in again. All of the crossings are easy, but some might be muddy because of horse or llama traffic—this is the route for llamas to carry food and laundry to Le Conte Lodge. Eight or 10 llamas make the trip twice a week, all roped together and led by a wrangler who lets the first llama in line carry his or her food and water. They move along fairly fast, but if you want to pass them from behind, just ask and they will oblige. From the trail high above a creek valley, you can look down into the tops of Eastern hemlocks, basswoods, and Fraser magnolias. After a little more than 1.0 mile from the trailhead, the trail rounds one more ridge, and you can hear a louder, more insistent creek. This is Roaring Fork, which roars and tumbles from near the top of Mt. Le Conte down to Gatlinburg, where it joins the West Prong of the Little Pigeon. As you approach Grotto Falls, look down to the left and watch the white water. A straight downhill section of trail takes you to Grotto Falls, with a little sign in case there's any doubt. There are rocks to rest on; Grotto Falls draws crowds on some days.

Liverworts grow in the rocks within the spray zone, and if it's warm, you should be able to see salamanders basking in misty showers. Upstream and down you can see massive boulders and throngs of rosebay rhododendron. Crossing Roaring Fork can be a little tricky as the stepping stone may be slippery. In very high water, crossing may be difficult or impossible.

Trillium Gap Trail after the falls is narrower and rockier, but still a good trail, climbing through mature forest. Near the seeps that cross the trail, giant yellow buckeyes and shaggy yellow birches grow. About 1.0 mile beyond the falls, a boulder field starts—great fractured rocks with polypody ferns and fabulous mosses. Trees and shrubs growing on these rocks have developed wild designs as their roots searched for soil. These boulders came from the extreme cold of the glacial periods. Though the glaciers apparently did not reach the Smokies, cold weather did, and water and deep freezing fractured off boulders from the bedrock.

A creek running through part of the boulder field is easy to cross but could be slippery. After the creek, the trail continues to rise and passes a wonderful rock face on the right decorated with white, yellow, and green lichens. Soon you might see a few red spruce cones on the trail and find red spruce among the Eastern hemlock. Then grass appears, and soon the open forest of gray, lichen-covered American beech trees. Look for a big gnarled silverbell tree on the left with clusters of root sprouts. Ahead, you can see the Trillium Gap sign and trail junction.

Trillium Gap is a typical American beech gap, with beech trees and grass as the dominant plants. They thrive here because they can withstand the constant wind. If you stand at the entrance of the spur trail to Brushy Mountain and look south toward Mt. Le Conte, you can see that the beech gap is roughly triangular, and you are standing in the center of one side. The triangle extends down both sides of the gap and ahead up the slope. However, the sharp rise of Brushy Mountain behind you offers some protection, and Eastern hemlocks, rosebay rhododendrons and a few young red spruce trees grow there.

Brushy Mountain is a heath bald knob on a slope of Mount Le Conte. Heath balds, or laurel slicks, occur on high elevation, exposed areas with thin, acidic soils. The dominant plants are in the heath family: mountain laurel, Catawba rhododendron, sand myrtle, blueberry, and wintergreen. From a distance, this growth looks smooth; hence the name bald or slick. On Brushy Mountain, the heath plants grow taller than most people and look brushy close up, but somehow the name Brushy Bald seems like an oxymoron.

To reach the top of Brushy Mountain, turn left at Trillium Gap and hike 0.4 mile up an eroded, rocky trail that doubles as a stream bed through Eastern hemlock, rosebay rhododendron, and a few red spruce. The trail enters first a rhododendron, then a mountain laurel tunnel. Near the top, galax, wintergreen, and trailing arbutus line the trail, and as it levels out, other heath family plants appear: sand myrtle, blueberry, and huckleberry. Sand myrtle is a knee-high shrub with shiny, leathery evergreen leaves the size of sunflower seeds. It

grows almost exclusively on high exposed knobs or ridges and produces tiny sweet-smelling white flowers in April or May and sometimes again in September.

The trail levels and provides great views for very tall people. But finally, you come to an opening (elevation 4,911') and can see the sharp rise of Mount Le Conte out of Trillium Gap and behind that, the backbone of the Smokies. If you are so inclined, from the far end of the heath bald you can also look out over Pigeon Forge, Sevierville, and the outskirts of Knoxville, usually recognizable by its halo of polluted air.

← *Grotto Falls*

MADDRON BALD

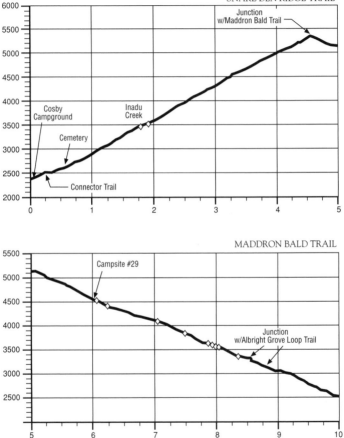

SNAKE DEN RIDGE TRAIL

Junction w/Maddron Bald Trail

Cosby Campground

Inadu Creek

Cemetery

Connector Trail

MADDRON BALD TRAIL

Campsite #29

Junction w/Albright Grove Loop Trail

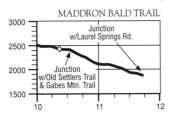

MADDRON BALD TRAIL

3000

2500

2000

1500

Junction
w/Laurel Springs Rd.

Junction
w/Old Settlers Trail
& Gabes Mtn. Trail

10   11   12

LENGTH: 9.6 miles roundtrip via Snake Den Ridge Trail or 11.8 miles one way going up Snake Den Ridge Trail and down Maddron Bald Trail (car shuttle required). Add 0.4 mile if going around Albright Grove loop.

HIGHLIGHTS: Views, big trees.

CAUTIONS: Some creek cross-ings on middle section of Maddron Bald. Snake Den Ridge is one of the steeper trails in the park.

MAP KEY: B 9-10; USGS quads: Hartford, Luftee Knob.

USE: Horse and hiking trail.

TRAILHEAD: To start on Snake Den Ridge Trail, go to the entrance to Cosby Campground and park in the hiker parking area. Walk into the campground to Campsite B-55 and look for a trail sign and gate.

To get to Maddron Bald Trailhead, drive on US 321 15.5 miles east from Gatlinburg or 2.8 miles west from Cosby to Baxter Road, which is 0.1 mile east of Yogi's Campground. Keep to the right until you reach Laurel Springs Road and the marked park trailhead at the park boundary. There is only room for four or five cars, and they may not be safe; several vehicles have been stolen from here and recycled at a local chop shop. Safe parking (for a fee) may be available at busi-nesses on U.S. 321. Do not park on private property without permis-sion.

Maddron Bald is a big heath bald, a giant hump sticking out on the north slope of the Great Smokies. Such shrubs as mountain laurel, rhododendron, blueberry bushes and mountain myrtle grow here.

The shortest way to it is by way of the Snake Den Ridge Trail out of Cosby Campground. The trail climbs to an old traffic circle at mile **0.7**. From a cement slab on the right you can look down at the creek. Just left of the cement slab, the trail passes three big boulders and becomes rocky as it rises above the creek. After it descends through a rocky old stream bed and approaches Rock Creek, you'll need to look

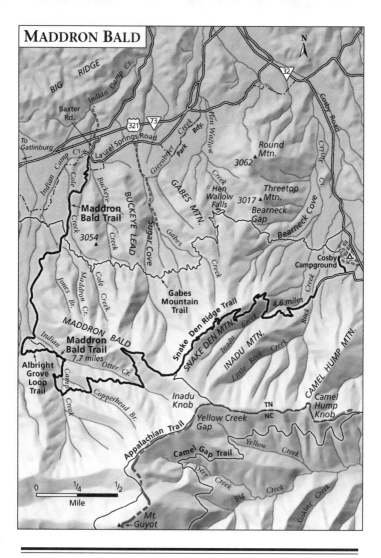

MADDRON BALD

for a new foot log upstream. After the creek, larger trees indicate that you have moved out of the settled area. Tuliptrees, silverbells, and Eastern hemlocks line the steep, rocky trail as it turns away from the creek. Look for a shattered Eastern hemlock stump on the left and for American chestnut logs and stumps throughout the woods.

The trail swings around a switchback at mile **1.4**. A big silverbell tree stands in the angle; look for flaky bluish bark. In April, silverbells carpet the trail with their flowers, and in September, they drop light brown winged nuts that are hard for anyone except squirrels to open.

After the switchback, the trail enters a jumble of boulders and an old stream bed. Foamflower, violets, nettles, and Fraser's sedge bloom here in spring, and jewelweed, goldenrod, and Indian cucumber bloom later.

After more steep climbing and another dry stream bed, the trail finally drops a little to cross Inadu Creek at about **1.8** miles. It is an easy crossing and has upstream and downstream waterfalls and a quiet pool with water striders.

The trail again heads away from the creek, supported by a strong rock wall on the right. But this time, the trail reaches the nose of the ridge. Through Eastern hemlocks, you can get a view into the valley, and then the vegetation changes to that characteristic of exposed ridges: mountain laurel, American beech, oak, maple, pine, with a ground cover of trailing arbutus, galax, wintergreen, and flat mosses. As the trail turns back to a more sheltered cove, rosebay rhododendron, Eastern hemlock, and Fraser magnolia dominate. Shining clubmoss, which looks like furry green fingers, grows below. The trail alternates between exposed and sheltered habitats. From one ridge nose, you can see Cosby Valley and Foothills Parkway, and if you lean out carefully, you can get a glimpse of Mt. Cammerer to the right.

By now you are above 4,000' elevation, and you start seeing small red spruce trees beside the trail, though Eastern hemlock is still the dominant conifer. After another switchback, the trail runs along the top of a dry ridge with a steep drop-off on both sides. Mountain laurel, Catawba rhododendron, wintergreen, ground pine (another clubmoss) and reindeer moss (a lichen) grow here. Then a mountain lau-

The Baxter cabin on Maddron Bald Trail.

rel and rosebay rhododendron tunnel closes over you as the trail slips off to the side of the ridge.

When you emerge from the tunnel, you will see more red spruce than Eastern hemlock. Hemlock needles are flat with a white line underneath; spruce needles are square in cross section with no white line. Other high elevation plants, such as hobblebush and mountain maple, grow here, along with large yellow birches. Spring-beauty, painted trillium, Clinton's lily, and rosy twisted-stalk are some of the flowers that bloom here in May.

The trail becomes level in a large grassy spot with a yellow buckeye tree in the middle at mile **4.2**. Moving along, the trail is rocky, narrow, and steep up to the Maddron Bald Trail junction at mile **4.6**. Turn right onto Maddron Bald Trail and descend slightly for about one-quarter mile to the bald.

Those wanting an alternate route down, provided they can arrange a second car at the end, can go down the Maddron Bald Trail 7.3 miles. The lower portion of it, in the valley of Indian Camp Creek, has some of the park's finest woodland. The Albright Grove Nature Trail loops off this trail. On it grow some huge trees, including two very large tuliptrees. Those wanting to start this trail from the lower end should drive about 16 miles eastward on U.S. 321 from the intersection of 321 and U.S. 441 in downtown Gatlinburg, then turn onto Baxter Road (just past Yogi's Campground) and keep to the right until you reach the park boundary and Maddron Bald Trailhead.

MIDDLE PRONG ~ GREENBRIER RIDGE

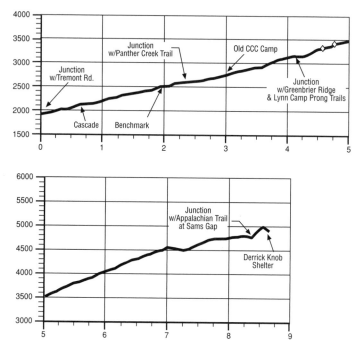

LENGTH: 4.6 miles roundtrip from the end of Tremont Road to the junction with Panther Creek Trail and back. 17.3 miles roundtrip from the end of Tremont Road to Derrick Knob Shelter on the Appalachian Trail and back.

HIGHLIGHTS: Waterfalls, wildflowers.

CAUTIONS: Two stream crossings may be difficult in high water.

MAP KEY: D-E 5; USGS quad: Thunderhead Mountain.

USE: Horse and hiking trails.

TRAILHEAD: Follow the signs from the Townsend "Y" toward

MIDDLE PRONG/GREENBRIER RIDGE TRAILS

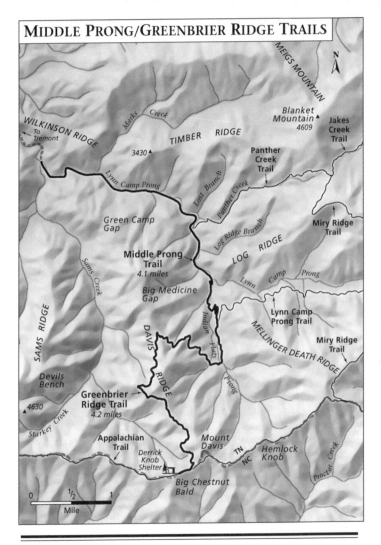

MEIGS MOUNTAIN

WILKINSON RIDGE
To Tremont

Marks Creek

TIMBER RIDGE

3430▲

Blanket Mountain ▲ 4609

Jakes Creek Trail

Panther Creek Trail

Lynn Camp Prong

Last Branch

Panther Creek

Green Camp Gap

Log Ridge Branch

LOG RIDGE

Miry Ridge Trail

Middle Prong Trail
4.1 miles

Sams Creek

Big Medicine Gap

Lynn Camp Prong

Lynn Camp Prong Trail

Miry Ridge Trail

SAMS RIDGE

DAVIS RIDGE

Indian Flats

MELLINGER DEATH RIDGE

Devils Bench

Greenbrier Ridge Trail
4.2 miles

Prong

▲ 4630

Starkey Creek

Appalachian Trail

Derrick Knob Shelter

Mount Davis

TN

NC

Hemlock Knob

Proctor Creek

Big Chestnut Bald

0   1/2   1
Mile

N

Cades Cove. In 0.2 mile, turn left onto the Tremont Road. At 2.3 miles, you will see the entrance to the Great Smoky Mountains Institute at Tremont, an environmental education camp, on your left. Continue on the main road, which quickly becomes a gravel road, and follow it for 3.1 miles to a gate and parking circle. The last three miles of this road are closed in winter.

There are shorter routes from the bottom to the top of the Great Smokies, but few are as interesting or on such an easy grade as this jaunt up Lynn Camp Prong and Davis Ridge.

Nearly every foot of the way is uphill, but easy uphill, not steep uphill. It is as if someone had built for you a gently-sloped ramp to the top of the mountain. The elevation gain over the 8.6 miles to Derrick Knob is nearly 3,000 feet.

It's a great wildflower hike, and late April is a good time to do it. It's also a hike of some historical interest, and nearly any time of year is good for history buffs.

From the gate at the end of Tremont Road, the left stream fork is Lynn Camp Prong and you will follow it along an old road (Middle Prong Trail) that rises gently with the stream. You may see blooms of sweet white violets, great chickweed, toothwort and trillium immediately after you start walking. Then you will come to one of the more unusual waterfalls in the park. Lynn Camp Prong's waters plunge, glide and cascade over a huge stone buff. The whole procedure covers many yards and is lovely to see.

Some 25-30 minutes after you start walking you will reach the site where a logging era splash dam once stood. Until fairly recently, remains of the old wooden structure stretched across Lynn Camp exactly where Marks Creek joins Lynn Camp. Loggers built such dams and let water rise in small lakes behind them. They rolled logs into the lake and then opened the dam spillway to let the water carry the logs downstream on the way to a sawmill.

Charles A. Cope of Rockford, Tennessee, did some of his growing up at the old logging village of Tremont, where his father Fred A.

A cascade on Lynn Camp Prong. →

Cope, and his maternal grandfather, Robert V. Woodruff, worked for Little River Lumber Co. I had always assumed that Little River Lumber Co. built the splash dam. But Cope says the lumber company did not build it. He said it was a weathered old dam when Little River was logging that area in the 1930s. Park Service files indicate the dam probably was built by the J. J. English Co. which selectively cut mostly large tulip poplar trees there between 1880 and 1900. This means this old dam has existed for over 100 years.

Charles Cope also once lived about a mile farther up Lynn Camp, at a logging village called String Town. It was strung out in a single line of houses beside the logging railroad. While Cope's father was working for Little River Lumber Co., he also was taking a correspondence course in electrical engineering. One result of this was that Fred Cope built an overshot waterwheel on Lynn Camp, connected it to a generator and provided electricity for the home.

About 2.3 miles from where you started hiking, you will reach the first intersection. A trail to the left crosses Lynn Camp and goes up Panther Creek toward Jakes Gap. Continue up the Middle Prong Trail. Occasionally you will see an old apple tree, indicating that people once lived along the creek.

The creek forks again, and the stream carrying the Lynn Camp name swings to the left away from you, and your trail follows a small stream called Indian Flats Prong. On a happy morning about 35 years ago, I discovered that brook trout (and no rainbow trout) lived above a waterfall on Indian Flats. They still live there, but it is illegal to fish for them now. However, that may change if the brook trout population increases enough to justify it.

At the next trail fork, 1.8 miles from the previous one, the Lynn Camp Prong Trail turns left and your trail, the Greenbrier Ridge Trail, is the one to the right. (Perhaps it should be called the Davis Ridge Trail, for the ridge was renamed Davis Ridge years ago to honor Mrs. Willis P. Davis, who suggested in 1923 that a national park be established in the Great Smokies. The crest of that ridge is named Mt. Davis, honoring her husband who was one of a group of men who participated in the long campaign for the park. The national park was officially established in 1934.)

Four and two-tenths more miles of walking up Davis Ridge will take you to the crest of the Smokies at Sams Gap. Along the route you will see a good stand of yellow birch and cherry trees and masses of wildflowers that include spring-beauties, dwarf ginseng, Dutchman's-breeches and squirrel corn. You'll even pass a ramp patch.

When you reach the crest of the Great Smokies at the Appalachian Trail, turn right and go 0.3 mile to Derrick Knob, where stands an AT shelter. It was near this shelter that another shelter stood many years ago. It was called the Hall Cabin. Hunters and herdsmen from Tennessee and North Carolina used it.

An unusual feature of the cabin was the dining table. There was a hole in the center of the table, and a chute extended from the hole down through the cabin floor. Diners dumped their table scraps down the chute to waiting hunting dogs under the floor.

MOUNT CAMMERER

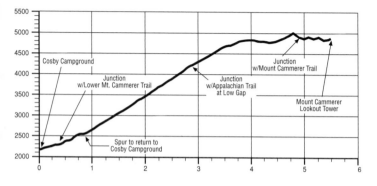

LENGTH: 11.2 miles roundtrip from Cosby Campground to the Mt. Cammerer lookout tower and back.

HIGHLIGHTS: Views from the Appalachian Trail and tower, big trees.

CAUTIONS: The A.T. and tower are not good places to be during lightning storms.

MAP KEY: 10 B; USGS quads: Hartford, Luftee Knob.

USE: Horse and hiking.

TRAILHEAD: Park at the designated hiker parking area near the entrance to Cosby Campground and near Cosby Picnic Area. Follow the Low Gap Trail to the Appalachian Trail.

A magnificent view from the top and the forest and flowers along the way make this long jaunt worthwhile. The altitude gain is over 2,700 feet—from 2,200 feet above sea level at the Cosby Campground starting point to 4,928 at Mt. Cammerer tower.

Though the grade is never extremely steep, this is a fairly difficult hike because you are nearly always ascending. There are few level stretches from the campground to Cammerer.

But the spring flowers and autumn colors make the trip well worthwhile during those seasons. And on any clear day, the view from

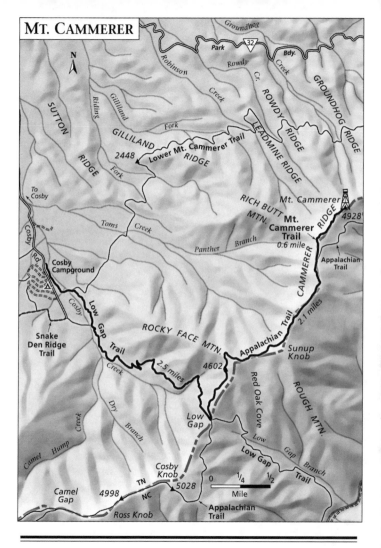

MT. CAMMERER

N

Groundhog
Park
32
Bdy.
Robinson
Rowdy
Cr.
Creek
ROWDY RIDGE
GROUNDHOG RIDGE
LEADMINE RIDGE

SUTTON RIDGE

Riding

Gilliland

Fork

GILLILAND RIDGE

Lower Mt. Cammerer Trail

2448

Gilliland
Fork

To Cosby

Toms   Creek

RICH BUTT MTN.

Mt. Cammerer

Mt.
Cammerer
Trail
0.6 mile

CAMMERER RIDGE

4928

Panther   Branch

Appalachian
Trail

Cosby
Rd.

Cosby Campground

2.1 miles

Cosby

Low Gap Trail

Snake Den Ridge Trail

ROCKY FACE MTN.

Creek

2.5 miles

4602

Appalachian Trail

Sunup Knob

ROUGH MTN.

Red Oak Cove

Dry   Branch

Creek

Low Gap

Low
Gap
Branch

Low Gap Trail

Camel Hump   Creek

Camel Gap

4998   TN
NC

Cosby Knob

5028

0   ¼   ½

Mile

Appalachian Trail

Ross Knob

Cammerer is worth the long walk.

Mt. Cammerer offers one of the two or three best views in the park. Some will tell you it's the best. The small fire lookout building perches on a high point of a rugged, treeless ledge of gray-white rock. (Because of the light color of the stone, which can be seen for miles, the peak once was called Whiterock.) Unlike the customary fire tower, with a cab atop a steel tower, this is a squat building of wood and stone.

Look from here at hundreds of square miles of fields and forests. To the north and east lie the farm lands of Cocke County, TN., with Pigeon River curving lazily through them. To the west runs the main range of the Great Smokies, with 6,621-foot Mt. Guyot, second highest peak in the park, dominating the scene. Stretching away to the south are the forested mountains of the North Carolina side of the park; another fire tower is visible on Mt. Sterling, five miles south.

Hike southward out of Cosby Campground 2.9 miles to Low Gap, then eastward slightly more than 2 miles on the Appalachian Trail to the Mt. Cammerer turn-off and 0.6 of a mile northward to the tower, for a one-way distance of about 5.6 miles. Sunup Knob and Rocky Face Mountain are on this stretch of the AT. Once when I was hiking alone between Low Gap and Rocky Face, I rounded a curve and met the biggest bobcat I ever saw. He unhurriedly ambled off into the woods, leaving the trail to me.

An alternate is a loop hike of about 16 miles that starts and ends in Cosby Campground. The first part is the same as the previous route: To Low Gap and east on the AT to Mt. Cammerer. Then follow the AT a little more than two miles east to the Lower Mt. Cammerer Trail. Follow that trail about 7.4 miles back to the campground. This is a great trail for wild iris, which bloom in the latter part of April and the first half of May. Look for a marker directing you off trail to the Sutton Ridge Overlook. It offers a good look at mountains to the north. Even more interesting is the fact that two unusually large American chestnut sprouts grow at this overlook.

← *The restored lookout tower atop Mt. Cammerer.*

MOUNT STERLING

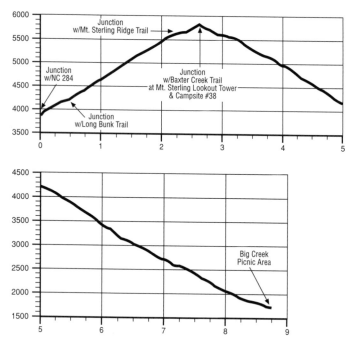

LENGTH: 5.4 miles roundtrip if you go up and down the Mount Sterling Trail. 8.8 miles one way going up Mt. Sterling Trail and down Baxter Creek Trail (car shuttle required).

HIGHLIGHTS: Views from Mt. Sterling tower, big trees on Baxter Creek Trail.

CAUTIONS: Both trails are very steep.

MAP KEY: C-B 11; USGS quad: Cove Creek Gap

USE: Horse and hiking trail.

TRAILHEAD: Mt. Sterling Gap. Access to the trailhead via I-40: In North Carolina use exit 20 onto route 276. Immediately turn right

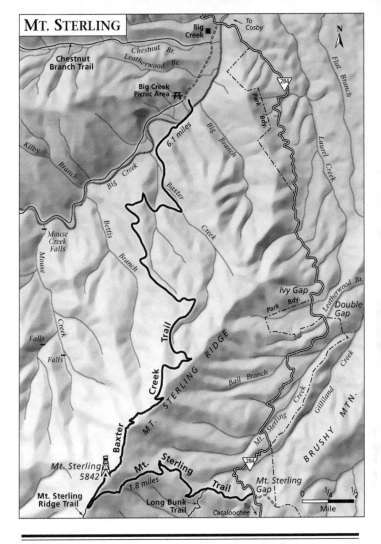

MT. STERLING

Big Creek

→ To Cosby

Chestnut Br.

Chestnut
Branch Trail

Leatherwood Br.

Big Creek
Picnic Area

N

284

Flat Branch

Kilby Branch

Big Creek

Baxter Creek

6.1 miles

Big Branch

Laurel Creek

Park Bdy.

Mouse
Creek
Falls

Bettis Branch

Creek Trail

MT. STERLING RIDGE

Ivy Gap

Park Bdy.

Leatherwood Br.

Double
Gap

Mouse Creek

Falls

Falls

Bail Branch

Gilliland Creek

Mt. Sterling Creek

BRUSHY MTN.

Baxter Creek Trail

Mt. Sterling
5842

Mt. Sterling

1.8 miles

Sterling Trail

284

Mt. Sterling Ridge Trail

Long Bunk
Trail

Mt. Sterling
Gap

To
Cataloochee

0   ¼   ½
Mile

onto Cove Creek Road (Old 284) and proceed 15.7 miles. In Tennessee use exit 451 (Waterville Road) off I-40. Turn left after crossing the Pigeon River and left again after 2.3 miles at the village of Mount Sterling. Follow old NC 284 toward Cataloochee for 6.8 miles to Mt. Sterling Gap.

Towering to an altitude of 5,842 feet between the valleys of Cataloochee and Big Creeks, Mt. Sterling is the highest peak so close to the eastern boundary of Great Smoky Mountains National Park.

After climbing high enough on the fire tower atop Sterling to see across the tops of the spruce and fir trees, you can see for miles in every direction. About five miles north and slightly west is the squat little fire-lookout building on Mt. Cammerer. Nearly eight miles west is Mt. Guyot, and 4.5 miles southwest is Big Cataloochee Knob. Sterling's peak is about 1.6 miles from the eastern boundary of the park.

But you don't walk a straight line to Mt. Sterling. The closest route from where a hiker can park his car is about two miles. This is the distance by way of the trail from old North Carolina Highway 284, at Mt. Sterling Gap, to the top of the mountain. It's a steep climb, with an altitude gain of 1,954 feet over the 2.7 miles.

The trail winds up Sterling's south slope. Oaks—especially northern red oaks—predominate along the first half of the route. Several silverbell trees usually provide a good show of bloom in late April and May. Patches of trailing arbutus, galax, and teaberry grow along the road banks.

If you can get someone to drive your car around to the Big Creek Picnic Area (just past the campground), the suggested route down from Mt. Sterling is 6.2 miles down the north slope by way of the Baxter Creek Trail to Big Creek.

The first part of the Baxter Creek Trail down from the top is through a spruce-fir forest high on the ridge crest. You'll notice many dead fir trees, victims of a pest known as the balsam wooly adelgid. Many other downed trees are victims of fierce winds that rip across the mountain's top. The narrow trail, exposed rock faces, and wind-ravaged trees lend this section a wonderfully wild feel.

Some two miles from the top, the trail forks. Take the left fork. (The other one is no longer maintained.)

Trillium, hepatica, spring-beauty, and partridgeberry are among the wildflowers that bloom along this trail.

The altitude drop over the 6.2 miles is more than 4,000 feet. So it's much less difficult to go down it than up it.

An interesting route to reach either starting point is by way of narrow, amazingly winding Tennessee Highway 32 from Cosby. It is paved, but at the North Carolina line, at Davenport Gap, the road changes to unpaved North Carolina 284. It is nearly 13 miles from Cosby to Big Creek (at the village of Mt. Sterling) and nearly 20 miles from Cosby to Mt. Sterling Gap.

OLD SETTLERS TRAIL

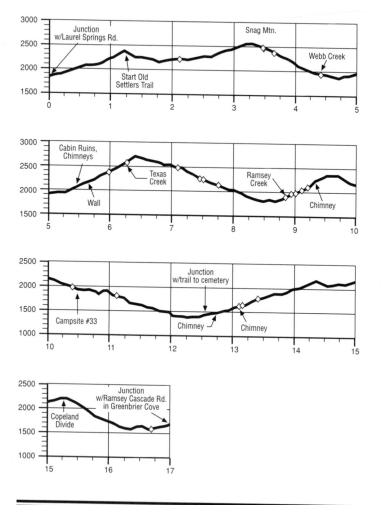

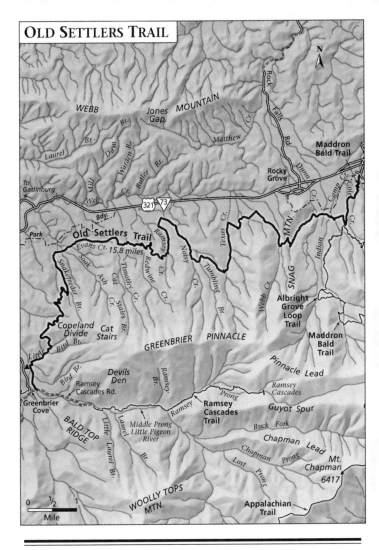

OLD SETTLERS TRAIL

N

WEBB MOUNTAIN

Jones Gap

Rock

Falls Rd.

Matthew

Maddron Bald Trail

Laurel Br.

Dam Br.

Warden Br.

Butler Br.

Mill Wall Cr.

Cr.

Rocky Grove

Dunn Cr.

To Gatlinburg

Bdy.

321 73

Camp Cr.

Cole Cr.

Park

Old Settlers Trail

Evans Cr. 15.8 miles

Ramsey Cr.

Noisy Cr.

Texas Cr.

MTN.

Snakefeeder Br.

Soak Ash Cr.

Cat Stairs Br.

Timothy Cr.

Redwine Cr.

Tumbling Br.

SNAG

Indian Cr.

Webb Cr.

Albright Grove Loop Trail

Copeland Divide

Bird Br.

Cat Stairs

GREENBRIER PINNACLE

Maddron Bald Trail

Littl

Bird Br.

Ramsey Cascades Rd.

Devils Den

Ramsey Br.

Pinnacle Lead

Ramsey Cascades

Greenbrier Cove

BALD TOP RIDGE

Little Laurel Br.

Laurel Br.

Middle Prong Little Pigeon River

Ramsey Prong

Ramsey Cascades Trail

Guyot Spur

Buck Fork

Chapman Lead

Chapman Prong

Lost Prong

Mt. Chapman 6417

WOOLLY TOPS MTN.

Appalachian Trail

0   ½   1
Mile

LENGTH: 17 miles one way from the Maddron Bald Trailhead near Cosby to Greenbrier Cove. A car shuttle is recommended.

HIGHLIGHTS: remnants of mountain farms—stone walls, chimneys, other relics.

CAUTIONS: some stream crossings may be difficult in high water.

MAP KEY: 8-9 C-B; USGS quads: Mt. Le Conte, Mt. Guyot, Jones Cove.

USE: hiking trail.

TRAILHEAD: Take U.S. 321 15.5 miles east from Gatlinburg or 2.8 miles west from Cosby to Baxter Road, which is 0.1 mile east of Yogi's Campground. Keep to the right on Baxter Road until you reach the marked Maddron Bald trailhead on the park boundary. There is only room for 4-5 cars, and they may not be safe from thieves. Safe parking (sometimes for a fee) may be available at nearby businesses on U.S. 321. Walk the Maddron Bald Trail 1.2 miles to the start of Old Settlers Trail.

This is a long walk: 17 miles across hills and narrow valleys and more than 100 years into the Great Smokies' past. Before the National Park was established over a half-century ago, many families lived in log homes and wrested a living from this stony land. A 1931 map shows more than 50 buildings in the foothills north of the Pinnacle Lead. Most of them were in an elevation range of 1,350 to 3,000 feet above sea level.

Small creeks named Indian Camp, Dunn, Webb, Texas, Noisy, Redwine, Timothy, Soak Ash and Copeland pour hurriedly down from the Pinnacle high country and then move leisurely through the area where the people lived. It was on the narrow bottoms along these creeks that mountain farmers planted most of their gardens and corn patches and grew hay for their livestock. But some did it the harder way and plowed the hillsides, setting them up for erosion.

Nearly all the narrow roads of dirt and stone went up the valleys and stopped at the last house in each valley. Though there were one or two exceptions, roads generally did not cross the dividing ridges to connect the valleys. The Park Service in more recent years rehabilitated portions of these old roads and connected them with trail segments across the ridges. These old roads and new trail connectors now comprise the Old Settlers Trail.

The Maddron Bald Trail starts at the park boundary. Follow that trail 1.2 miles to its intersection with the Gabes Mountain Trail to the east and the Old Settlers Trail to the west. The cabin you pass along the way was built by members of the Baxter family in 1889. The 16' x 18' cabin has no windows or porch, but at one time included a kitchen lean-to on the west side and a sleeping loft. Alex and Sara Baxter raised four children in this tiny home.

You'll come to the next historic site within 10 minutes of turning west onto the Old Settlers Trail. The most visible part still standing is a portion of the old stone chimney. If you make this hike in winter, you will see more of the old ruins than if you do it in summer when tall weeds and tree leaves hide some of them.

In March and April, daffodils mark some places where families once lived; old-fashioned roses do the same for others in June. But it is stone that marks them in all seasons. Stone chimneys, stone foundations, stone fences, stone retaining walls. And piles of stones that served no purpose. The piles are there because this area has an over-abundance of rocks. After using them for chimneys, walls and fences, the farmers had rocks left over. So they gathered them from the land they intended to cultivate and left them in piles.

After walking about a mile, you will find yourself going south up a pleasant little valley. On and on the trail goes parallel to a small stream and sometimes crossing it. You see a homesite here and there. Finally, the trail climbs out of the valley and up and over a hill called Snag Mountain. Mountain laurel blooms on Snag Mountain in June.

Your next stream is a small unnamed tributary of Webb Creek. It may be dry if there has been no recent rain. Then comes Webb Creek, on your left as you walk generally northward. You will see stone walls on both sides of the creek. Finally, you come to the stream crossing, with Old Settlers Trail markers on both sides of Webb Creek. But if you have a little time to spare, don't cross just yet. Instead, follow the old road you will see curving to your right beside an old stone wall. Walk this road a few more than 100 paces to another road. Turn left for only four or five paces and then turn right again.

You will be looking at the Tyson McCarter barn, one of the old pre-park buildings the Park Service has selected to maintain. As you draw nearer you also will see the McCarter springhouse.

I talked with Ollie McCarter Ramsay, who was born April 8, 1904, in the log dwelling whose ruins stand near the barn and springhouse. "Tyson McCarter was my pappy," she said.

"My daddy used to say his boys were all girls." She said this meant that she and her four sisters (a fifth sister "died young") had to work just like boys. Among the jobs they did was load big rocks on a sled which their mules pulled to the place where her uncle Harrison McCarter would build them into a sturdy fence. Harrison McCarter also built stone chimneys.

Ollie said her family owned two mules, two cows, two hogs, as well as small flocks of chickens, ducks and geese. They grew corn, wheat, rye and tobacco. Most of these crops, including the tobacco, were for home consumption. She said the men "chewed tobacco like worms." Adding to their near self-sufficiency was a big apple orchard and a smaller peach orchard.

"All the people around us were poor," Ollie said. "But they got along better than we do now. They loved each other then." Ollie's husband, Perry Ramsay, 89 years old when I talked with them, also was born inside what's now the park and also in the valley of Webb Creek. In the 66th year of their marriage, they said they'd never considered a divorce. However, she joked, "I've felt like whipping him."

Retrace your steps back to the Old Settlers Trail. Cross Webb Creek this time, and your route soon will take you along an old, old road between two stone fences. The fence on your left is particularly impressive, more than six feet high in places and about three feet thick. It was built to last and it has.

After leaving Webb Creek Valley, you follow the trail high into the headwaters of Texas Creek. This probably is the most strenuous portion of the trail, as you climb from an altitude of about 2,000 feet to 3,000 feet. You cross seven or eight tributaries of Texas Creek, plus the main stream. Up near the 3,000-foot mark, on the upper side of the trail, are the ruins of a larger-than-usual mountain home. Proof of this are two chimneys still standing. Most homes in this area had only one chimney.

After leaving Texas Creek Valley, the trail takes you into the valley of Noisy Creek. You first cross Tumbling Branch, a tributary to Noisy. Then comes Noisy, which you cross twice. An old homesite is to the right of the first crossing. Civil War veteran Sam Ramsay, grandfather of Perry Ramsay, built the house that first stood there and his family was the first to live in it. Immediately to the left of the second crossing is a stone retaining wall built to protect the house that stood there from the creek in flood. Notice the inverted-V stone lintel atop the fireplace. You have seen this type lintel over other fireplaces on this trail and you will see others like it before you finish the hike. You wonder whether the same stonemason did them all. The Thornton Jenkins family lived here.

About a half-mile west of the last crossing of Noisy Creek is a trail fork. Your route, the Old Settlers Trail, is the left fork. The one to the right goes down the left side of Noisy Creek to Highway 321, about a mile away. The Park Service does not maintain it.

About a half-mile west of the trail fork is a high stone fence, on the left side of the trail, and behind it stands a tall stone chimney. It also has the inverted-V lintel.

On one early June hike I saw early-blooming rosebay rhododendron on this trail. A heavy mountain laurel bloom was past its peak. Many little pipsissewa plants were blooming, and I saw one beautiful rosebud orchid bloom. Heavier-than-normal rainfall had brought out lots of colorful mushrooms.

Ramsey Creek is the next one west of Noisy and the trail crosses it four or five times. Then comes Redwine Creek and, shortly later, backcountry campsite 33, at the site of an old home.

About a half-mile west of the campsite, the trail runs between an old corncrib, on the left, and a chimney, on the right. Part of an old Dutch oven rested near the chimney the last time I was there. This was the home of the Elmer Proffitt family, according to one of the sons, Ellis, who lives not so far away, down on Highway 321. His mother's roses still bloom at the old home site.

Cross Timothy Creek shortly after leaving the Proffitt place.

Then walk down a long hill into a different kind of country: Flat bottoms along a slower stream, a stream with cut banks, rather than rocky sides. This is Cat Stairs Branch. Tall corn probably grew here many decades ago; tall weeds grow in the rich bottomland now.

Soon you will leave the flat low country and begin the long, gradual ascent of Copeland Divide. Scattered flame azaleas bloom in season on Copeland Divide. So does goat's-beard, a tall plant with long, creamy-white flowers.

Once over the divide, you've finished your hard hiking for the day. Cross Little Bird Branch and expect to see Little River's Middle Prong, far down below, within 12 to 15 minutes. Look for wild iris blooms along the way in April and May.

Cross a small unnamed tributary of Bird Branch, then Bird Branch itself. The rest of the way to the car is an easy walk across flat country. Enjoy.

RAMSEY CASCADES

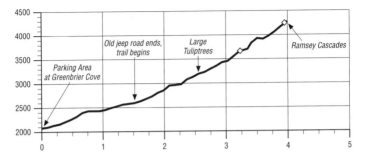

Parking Area at Greenbrier Cove

Old jeep road ends, trail begins

Large Tuliptrees

Ramsey Cascades

LENGTH: 8 miles roundtrip from Greenbrier Cove to the waterfall and back.

HIGHLIGHTS: Waterfall, big trees.

CAUTIONS: Do not climb on rocks around waterfall. Several fatalities have occurred at this location.

MAP KEY: 8-9 C; USGS quad: Mt. Guyot.

USE: Hiking trail.

TRAILHEAD: From the intersection of U.S. 441 and 321 in downtown Gatlinburg, follow 321 east about six miles to the Greenbrier entrance to the national park. Turn right and follow a narrow park road up-stream past the Greenbrier ranger station. Look for a Ramsey Cascade marker where the road forks, one road continuing up the right side of the stream and the other turning abruptly left across the stream. Yours is the one to the left.

Here's a drive and then a walk through a forest of big trees and along lively streams. The drive is along Middle Prong of Little Pigeon River. The walk is partly along Middle Prong and partly along one of its tributaries, Ramsey Prong. The destination is one of the most refreshing places in the mountains on a hot summer day.

Your hike starts at a small parking area on the right side of the road, just before you reach a pedestrian bridge over Middle Prong.

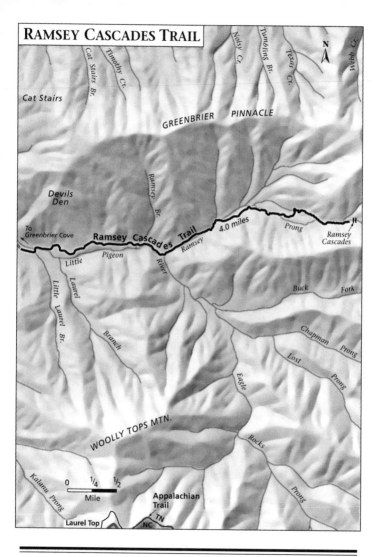

RAMSEY CASCADES TRAIL

Cat Stairs Br.

Timothy Cr.

Noisy Cr.

Tumbling Br.

Texas Cr.

Webb Cr.

N

Cat Stairs

GREENBRIER PINNACLE

Devils
Den

Ramsey Br.

To Greenbrier Cove

Ramsey Cascades Trail

4.0 miles

Prong

Ramsey
Cascades

Little

Pigeon

Ramsey

Little Laurel Br.

Laurel

River

Buck

Fork

Branch

Chapman

Prong

Lost

Prong

Eagle

WOOLLY TOPS MTN.

Rocks

Prong

Kalanu Prong

0   1/4   1/2
Mile

Appalachian
Trail

TN

Laurel Top

NC

This is a moderately difficult hike, steep and stony. You gain about 2,140 feet in altitude.

However, the first 1.5 miles of the hike is along an old road and is reasonably easy. When you come to the end of this road, you'll see the marker for the trail that will take you up along the stream called Ramsey Prong to Ramsey Cascade.

Except for a stretch of about one-half mile, the trail winds close to the stream, and hikers will enjoy some lovely mountain stream scenes. They also will notice other scenes typical of these high mountain valleys, with their heavy rainfall and temperate climate.

See how quickly ferns and other small plants and even trees start growing on fallen tree trunks—on some even before they fall. After crossing the second footbridge turn and look back at the horizontal branch of the tree growing near the other end of the bridge. Though it is 10 to 12 feet above ground, it is covered with ferns—sort of an aerial fernery.

You'll soon be walking in the largest section of old-growth forest in the Great Smokies. You'll see large tuliptrees, hemlocks and some big black cherries. Many of the larger trees are to be seen from the trail section between the two foot bridges, where the stream is to the left of the trail. You'll see them towering into the sky 100 or more yards from the trail. But you'll come to three big tulip trees right on the trail, within a few yards of each other. The largest of these is one of the half-dozen largest known trees in the park.

Look for trees with "prop roots." Many years ago, a seed sprouted in an old tree stump. Roots of the new tree grew through the old stump to the ground. Gradually the stump decayed, leaving the new tree with its roots extending two or three feet above ground. Also, look at trees that similarly grew from seeds that sprouted on large rocks. Unlike the stumps, the rocks did not decay. So the tree roots, like claws, clutch the rocks.

Ramsey Cascade is a high and mighty splash of white water down a craggy-faced ledge which is nearly vertical and about 90 feet high. It hits a dozen rocky noses and chins on the way down and pauses at none of them. It tempers its pace on a broad stone ledge, a few feet above where the trail meets the creek at the foot of the falls. The

ledge is a wonderful place to lie on one's back in the sunshine and be sprinkled with chilling spray from the cascading water. The ledge itself is refreshingly cool to the skin on a hot summer day. The view down the narrow green valley is pleasant. So is the view of the white water crashing down over the rocks above.

Climb no further, though. At least four people have lost their lives trying to climb this waterfall. Think how many hours away medical help is even if you only sprained an ankle.

On your return, count about 50 long paces from the second foot bridge across Ramsey Prong and then look uphill to your right. About 50 yards up in the woods is an old silver-sided snag of a dead chestnut tree. Measuring approximately 19 feet in circumference at chest height, this is one of the largest old chestnut tree trunks still standing in the park.

← *Ramsey Cascades*

Shuckstack

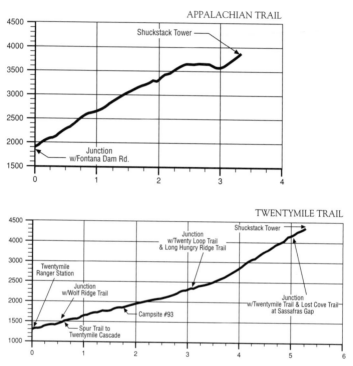

APPALACHIAN TRAIL

Shuckstack Tower

Junction
w/Fontana Dam Rd.

TWENTYMILE TRAIL

Shuckstack Tower

Junction
w/Twenty Loop Trail
& Long Hungry Ridge Trail

Twentymile
Ranger Station

Junction
w/Wolf Ridge Trail

Campsite #93

Junction
w/Twentymile Trail & Lost Cove Trail
at Sassafras Gap

Spur Trail to
Twentymile Cascade

LENGTH: 7.0 miles roundtrip via the Appalachian Trail; 8.9 miles one way via the Appalachian and Twentymile trails (car shuttle required); 10.8 miles roundtrip via Twentymile Trail.
HIGHLIGHTS: Views.
CAUTIONS: Fallen leaves can make sections of this steep route slippery.
MAP KEY: 3 F; USGS quad: Fontana Dam.
USE: Horse and hiking trail.

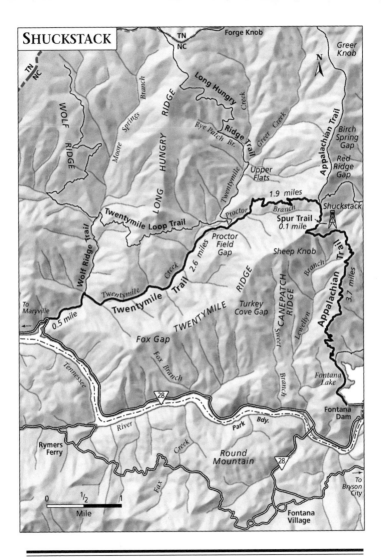

TRAILHEAD (Appalachian Trail): Drive or walk across Fontana Dam and take the road that forks to the right for 0.7 mile to the Appalachian Trail. **(Twentymile Trail):** The trailhead is located between Fontana Dam and Deals Gap on Highway 28. From most areas, access is via infamously slow, winding Highway 129.

High school and college football players wanting legs and lungs at their best in September might try getting summer jobs in the Fontana Dam section. A daily hike up Shuckstack Mountain will remove surplus pounds, build leg power and multiply stamina.

But if you're a middle-aged adult with cardiac troubles, rest often when you climb Shuckstack. Or ride a horse. However, adults in good physical condition should experience no trouble with it.

The 2,100-foot altitude gain from Fontana Dam to the top of Shuckstack used to be made over a 2.5-mile trail which mounted steep places the most direct way, climbing contour lines like stairsteps. The trail used now is easier but about three-quarters of a mile longer.

The trail is excellent for wildflowers. On a day in late April, I saw three species of trillium; three or four species of violets, including the lovely birdfoot violet; dogwood; silverbell and many less showy flowers.

Two or three weeks later, I could have seen mountain laurel blooming near the top of Shuckstack. It grows thickly along a narrow, rocky spine east of the top of Shuckstack. The old trail followed this spine.

To reach the old fire tower atop Shuckstack you must depart the A.T. where it turns to the left. The 0.1 mile spur trail to the tower is usually not well marked. It continues straight along the ridge where the A.T. turns.

Only about 4,000 feet above sea level, Shuckstack is not as high as several other peaks in the Great Smokies. But it is positioned in a way to give outstanding views to those who climb it.

To the north lies the main range of the Great Smokies, visible for a stretch of some 30 miles—from west of Gregory Bald eastward to Clingmans Dome. On a clear day, the Gregory and Spence Field grass balds are easily distinguishable. So is the ragged western slope of Mt. Buckley, just west of Clingmans.

Turn to the southwest. Down there is Fontana Lake, lying like a green dragon between the mountains, stretching appendages up narrow tributary valleys. Look to the southwest, where a portion of Cheoah Lake can be seen.

Let your eyes rove the mountains south of the Little Tennessee River Valley, the ranges of the Cheoah and Snowbird Mountains. Southward, on a line a little to the east of Fontana Dam, is Wauchecha Bald, 4,385 feet above sea level. It is one of the prominent Cheoah peaks.

If you're in a hurry, you can retrace your steps to the dam, for a 7-mile round trip. However, if you can arrange to have transportation waiting, you can follow the A.T. to Twentymile Trail and descend by it to the old Twentymile Ranger Station. You'll enjoy a 5.4-mile return to State Highway 28, where Twenty-Mile Creek pours into Cheoah Lake. Much of this route is by a trail once used by park motor vehicles. The grade is much easier than you followed from the dam to the mountaintop. The final 3-mile stretch parallels the creek and passes Twenty-Mile Ranger Station, only a few yards from the highway.

Twenty-Mile Creek gets its name from the fact that the distance is 20 miles from its mouth to the mouth of Hazel Creek. It's a good rainbow trout stream. Deep pools, cascades and falls also make it a delightfully pretty creek. Watch for a marker which will direct you to a particularly pretty cascade.

Twentymile Ranger Station is located in a remote area between Deals Gap and Fontana Village on Highway 28. During the warmer months you may want to access this area via one-way Parson Branch Road out of Cades Cove.

Some may prefer to do this hike in reverse—starting up Twenty-Mile Creek and descending the steep part to the dam.

SINKS TO JAKES CREEK

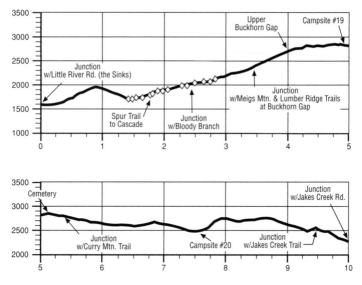

LENGTH: 10 miles one way from The Sinks on Little River Road to the trailhead for Jakes Creek near Elkmont Campground. A car shuttle is recommended.

HIGHLIGHTS: Waterfalls, wildflowers.

CAUTIONS: There are over 20 stream crossings, making this a better warm weather than cold weather hike.

MAP KEY: 5 C; USGS quads: Gatlinburg, Wear Cove.

USE: Horse and hiking trail.

TRAILHEAD: Drive to The Sinks parking area (sign post #5), 12 miles west of Sugarlands Visitor Center on Little River Road, or 6.0 miles east of the Townsend "Y" on the same road. The trail begins on the right side (closest to the river) of the parking area.

This hike on the Meigs Creek and Meigs Mountain trails starts at

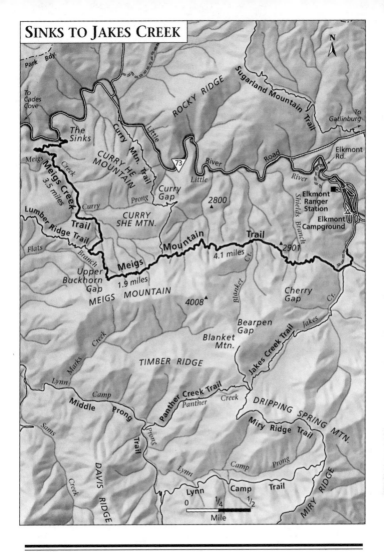

SINKS TO JAKES CREEK

N

the parking area at the Sinks, that spectacular pool in Little River, beside the Little River Road, between Townsend and Gatlinburg. The Meigs Creek Trail climbs first over a western lead of Curry He Mountain and then dips down into Meigs Creek Valley and follows this delightful little stream for a mile or more. A fine forest of large trees, many of them hemlocks, grow here. Look for a lovely, large beech tree to left of trail.

The trail leaves the valley and climbs to Buckhorn Gap, where it intersects the Lumber Ridge Trail to the west and the Meigs Mountain Trail to the east. The Lumber Ridge Trail is a 4-mile link to the Great Smoky Mountains Institute at Tremont. But for this hike, you take the Meigs Mountain Trail eastward. Within a mile, you'll reach Upper Buckhorn Gap, unmarked the last time I was there. If you are alert, you will notice an abandoned trail to the right. After you pass Backcountry Campsite 19, start looking to your left for an old cemetery some 20 yards off trail. This is Meigs Mountain Cemetery. where 22 former members of the Meigs Mountain community are buried. Most of the tombstones bear no names. Only two of them are commercial stones. A one-room school-church once stood nearby.

Next on your left will be Curry Mountain Trail, a route that leads three miles north to Little River Road. The trail reaches the road and the river just upstream from the Metcalf Bottoms Picnic Area. This trail once was a narrow road that served the people of Meigs Mountain community. More than 50 years ago, farmers grew crops and raised livestock in this area that is now all forest. In the late fall of 1988, I counted 50 fence posts still standing on the east side of the old road. Walk this old road some day; it's interesting. But today, continue right on the Meigs Mountain Trail, looking for old stone fences and other indications of long-ago farming.

As you near the end of the hike, you'll notice through the trees a small clearing on your left. A path branches from the trail and leads down to the clearing. This once was the farm and home of Lem Ownby. Lem died in early 1984. He was nearly 95 years old and had

← The Sinks

lived 93 years of that time on this 44-acre farm. (He was born and spent the first two years of his life a mile away.)

Lem was the last to die of a group of Great Smoky dwellers who chose to accept a little less money for their land when it was bought for the park in exchange for the right to live out their lives on that land. He once grew crops on this land, pastured cattle on it and sold honey from 145 bee hives that stood near his house. But as Lem's long life wound down gradually and gracefully, his eyes failed. His farm activities lessened year by year. The wilderness closed in a circle around him.

Young tuliptrees sprouted where Lem had grown corn. Within a few years, wilderness will take the last acre Lem left.

You may go down the path to Lem's old homesite and on down to the Jakes Creek Road, where you should have transportation waiting. Or you can continue on the regular trail, across Jakes Creek to the Jakes Creek Trail, and then left down that trail 0.4 mile to your car at the trailhead.

Spence Field & Thunderhead

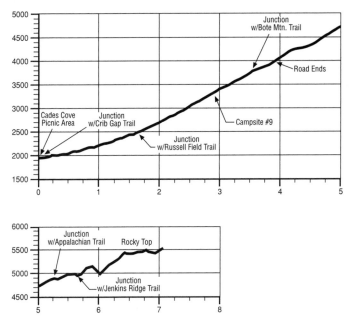

LENGTH: 14.2 miles roundtrip from Cades Cove Picnic Area to Thunderhead Mountain and back.

HIGHLIGHTS: Grassy balds, mountain views.

CAUTIONS: This is a difficult hike. You'll need to get an early start to finish before dark.

MAP KEY: 4E; USGS quad maps: Cades Cove, Thunderhead Mtn.

USE: Horse & hiking

TRAILHEAD: Start on Anthony Creek Trail which originates at Cades Cove Picnic Area. Parking is limited in the picnic area, so you may need to park at the campground store or parking area at the start of the loop road.

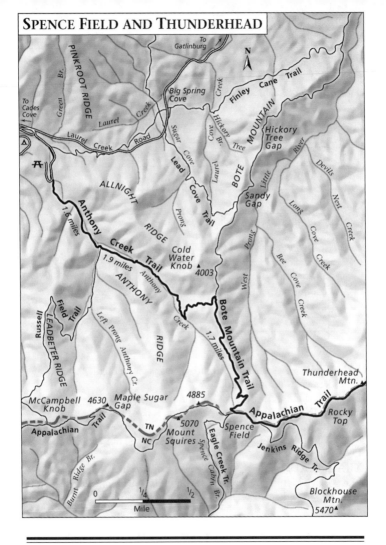

SPENCE FIELD AND THUNDERHEAD

To Gatlinburg

N

PINKROOT RIDGE

Green Br.

Laurel Creek

To Cades Cove

Laurel Creek Road

Big Spring Cove

Finley Cane Trail

Sugar Cove

Hickory Br.

Cove Br.

Laurel

Hickory Tree

BOTE MOUNTAIN

Hickory Tree Gap

Little River

Devils Nest Creek

ALLNIGHT RIDGE

Lead Cove Trail

Prong

Sandy Gap

Long Cove Creek

Anthony Creek Trail

1.6 miles

1.9 miles

Cold Water Knob
4003

Anthony Creek

West Prong

Bee Cove Creek

ANTHONY RIDGE

Bote Mountain Trail

1.7 miles

Field Trail

Russell

LEADBETTER RIDGE

Left Prong Anthony Cr.

Thunderhead Mtn.

McCampbell Knob   4630

Maple Sugar Gap

4885

Appalachian Trail

Rocky Top

Appalachian   Trail

TN

NC

5070
Mount Squires

Spence Field

Jenkins Ridge Tr.

Burnt Ridge Br.

Spence Cabin Br.

Eagle Creek Tr.

Blockhouse Mtn.
5470

0   1/4   1/2

Mile

192

Some hike to find solitude in still forests. Others look for natural beauty. A few want to match their muscles and stamina against these long trails to the highlands. This jaunt to Spence Field and Thunderhead Mountain fills all these purposes.

Your trail is the Anthony Creek Trail, which starts at the upper end of the Cades Cove Picnic Area. You will follow it 3.6 miles to an intersection with the Bote Mountain Trail. Turn right on the Bote Mountain Trail and follow it about 1.7 miles to the Appalachian Trail at Spence Field. Your beginning trail stays close to Anthony Creek, a small stream that sings along between flower-bordered banks. Anthony Creek Valley has some big tuliptrees, hemlocks, basswoods and other cove hardwood trees. Look for a particularly large hemlock, to the right of the trail, about one-half mile beyond the one-log foot bridge. Then, on the left side, about a half-mile farther, notice a large hemlock whose root system is arched like a foot over a big rock.

It's a good trail for wildflowers. Trillium is outstanding and comes in at least six different species. Prettiest is painted trillium. Its three petals are mostly white but are tinted rose-pink near the base. This trillium is most common at the higher elevations. You'll see it first on this trail 3,800 to 4,000 feet above sea level.

Spence Field has changed dramatically since the National Park Service took over the Great Smokies more than a half-century ago. In the 1930s, Spence was the largest grassy bald in the mountains. Oldtimers said it spread over more than 200 acres. In addition to Spence proper, this probably included a narrow grassy band eastward to Thunderhead.

In the years before the area became a park, cattle, sheep and horses grazed on the balds. Tom Sparks, whose winter home was in Cades Cove, was a herder from April to Labor Day. He lived in a cabin on Spence. He was responsible for about 600 cattle, 100 young horses and mules and about 1,000 sheep that grazed over an area from Thunderhead westward over Spence Field, Little Bald, and Russell Field. For his season-long herding services he charged $2 each for horses, $1.50 for cattle and 25 cents each for sheep. A steer eating the rich mountain grass would gain 300 to 400 pounds from April to September.

Since the Park Service banned grazing in the mountains soon after the area became a park, the encroaching forest has pinched Spence down from more than 200 acres to less than 30 acres. And the appearance of the remaining acres has changed.

Visitors now are not so much impressed by acres of grass as they are by a big natural orchard of serviceberry trees. When these show their white bloom in May, Spence is one of the loveliest scenes in the mountains. Some people like the slightly bitter flavor of the small red berries that come later. These trees on Spence have wide sturdy crowns, more like apple trees than like the slender serviceberry trees that grow in the more crowded forest.

I can't say exactly where Spence Field ends and Thunderhead Mountain begins. But 1.8 miles and four peaks—with deep saddles between them—separate the Spence Field and Thunderhead markers. Thunderhead is 5,527 feet above sea level. So the net altitude gain over Spence Field is only 569 feet. However, you climb nearly three times that much, only to lose most of it in the saddles between the peaks. While Spence Field is a grass bald, the top of Thunderhead is a heath bald. A few struggling trees grow at some points between the two.

One of the peaks between Spence Field and Thunderhead is called Rocky Top. When you see the jumble of broken gray rocks, you'll understand why.

Views from the peaks are worth the climb. Down south are pieces of Fontana Lake, like jigsaw puzzle pieces of a jade dragon. A finger of lake arrowing back toward you is Eagle Creek embayment. Lakes to be seen in the distance include Chilhowee, Douglas and maybe Fort Loudoun.

Then, there are good views of Cades Cove's emerald meadows. Stretching down and away on all sides are the mountains, clothed in dark green of hemlock and pine and lighter green of deciduous forest. Clouds constantly change the light pattern on the hills.

Rest while you look, and the trail back will be easier.

← *The view from Thunderhead.*

SELF-GUIDING NATURE TRAILS

While the longest park trails require days to complete, some outstandingly good ones take only a few minutes to an hour. These are the self-guiding nature trails, selected by park naturalists for their interesting natural history, beauty and accessibility.

Purchase an information leaflet from the box at the beginning of each trail. Numbered paragraphs in the leaflet match numbered guide posts along the trails. You can drive to within a few yards of the start of each trail. Most trails are irregular loops that come back to within a few feet of where they start.

BALSAM MOUNTAIN NATURE TRAIL
About 0.5 mile one way

This delightful little trail starts just inside the Balsam Mountain Campground, reached by way of a spur road off the Blue Ridge Parkway. It is a one-way trail. When you reach the last marker on the trail, you may continue on up to the paved road and take that route back to the campground, or you may return the way you came and expect to see some small treasure you missed the first time.

Following the trail, you walk through two types of high-country forest. First is a forest of widely-spaced deciduous hardwoods, dominated by beeches, birches and maples. Next is a darker spruce-fir forest. Actually, it now is mostly spruce because most of the Fraser firs have been killed by the balsam wooly adelgids.

Notice wild mountain grass that grows under the hardwoods. Before the park was established, cattle grazed in such areas. If you visit in late April or May, you cannot help noticing the areas of pink-white spring-beauty blooms, mixed with a few trout lilies and violets. The spring-beauties bloom and mature before the trees put out leaves to shade them.

CADES COVE NATURE TRAIL
0.75 mile roundtrip

This trail, off the Cades Cove loop road, gives you a look at a forest quite unlike what you see on the Cove Hardwood Trail.

Inexpensive brochures are available for each nature trail.

Here is a dry type forest. Pines and oaks predominate. Chestnuts once thrived here. The chestnut sprouts growing from the roots of the old dead trees will become victims of the chestnut blight before they grow very large.

Other tree species that share this forest include red maple, dogwood, several hickories and sourwood. From the tiny urn-shaped flowers of the sourwood flows nectar from which bees make the lightest-colored, best-flavored honey in the mountains. And from crooked-trunked sourwood trees East Tennessee mountaineers once made sled runners.

Bears—and humans—find huckleberries in this type forest.

COSBY NATURE TRAIL
0.75 mile roundtrip

Entrance to this trail is near the Cosby Campground Amphitheater. It is a good wildflower trail. Notice, especially, the thick mats of partridgeberry. This ground-hugging little plant extends its area by runners and suckers. It has tiny evergreen leaves. Twin flowers appear in the middle of spring, and its berries redden in autumn.

COVE HARDWOOD NATURE TRAIL
Less than 0.75 mile roundtrip

This trail winds through a magnificent cove hardwood forest. It has one of the best wildflower displays in the mountains each spring. Part of the forest is second-growth woodland, trees 50 or more years old. However, less than a mile from a highway traveled by millions each year, the trail will lead you into primeval forest, wilderness that has changed very little in thousands of years.

The trail begins just inside the Chimneys Picnic Area, off the Newfound Gap Road. Take a leaflet from the box, leave 50¢ and begin a rewarding walk in an area that is part pristine forest and part second-growth forest. Hardy mountaineers once grew corn and potatoes on portions of it.

This section of the Great Smokies is called Sugarlands, because East Tennesseans years ago tapped the numerous sugar maples that grow here and made maple sugar from the sap.

You'll pause by trees that have claw marks of bears which stood tall on their hind legs and raked the bark with their front claws for reasons best known only to the bears.

Among the tree species you'll see on this trail are eastern hemlocks, tuliptrees, basswood, buckeye, white ash, sugar maple, silverbell, yellowwood and black locust. More about the last three:

The largest black locust in the park once thrived on this trail but it was severely damaged in a storm. Mountain farmers made fence posts from long-lasting locusts. Bees make good honey from the nectar of their blooms.

The silverbell gets its name from the delicate bell-shaped white flowers that usually open in May, about the time dogwood blooms. It's one of the prettiest trees in the mountains then.

Even within its restricted range, the yellowood is rare ("Knowing Your Trees," published by the American Forestry Association, says it grows naturally only in the mountains of East Tennessee and Kentucky and Northern Alabama and in a small area of North-eastern Arkansas and Southern Missouri.) However, it is common along this trail, where you can see several. It blooms in May, and the white wisteria-like flowers are beautiful. It doesn't bloom every year, though. Some years it blooms, others it doesn't, without definite pattern.

April is the best time for the small wildflowers that grow on the floor of this forest, and the second half of April usually is better than the first half. Nevertheless, you may see hepaticas leading off the wildflower parade as early as February. However, they usually restrain themselves till March.

April finds the forest floor here nearly covered with fringed phacelia, a low-growing plant with small white flowers. The phacelia makes room for several species of violets, at least three of trillium, along with spring-beauties, trout lilies, Dutchman's breeches, squirrel corn, bishop's cap, wood anemone, puttyroot orchid and others.

ELKMONT NATURE TRAIL
0.8 mile roundtrip

This is another trail through a logged area. Most of the timber was cut more than 70 years ago. The land was cultivated for a time. Then it was bought for the park. Nature is reclaiming it. First came the high "weeds" and blackberries. Pine trees generally were next to grow here. Then came hardwoods, which eventually will dominate the area suited to their growth. But pines, oaks and heath plants probably will continue to reign on the southern exposure.

The trail area is in Mids Branch Valley. The branch is a tributary to Little River. Running along the slope of one side of the valley, crossing the valley and returning along the opposite slope, the trail gives you a look at two distinct forest types.

A young cove hardwood forest grows on the relatively moist northern exposure. Tuliptrees are numerous. On the southern exposure, on the opposite side of the valley, the principal trees are pines and oaks. They don't grow as close together as the trees on the other side. There's plenty of in-between space for laurel and rhododendron. Galax, trailing arbutus and teaberry plants are abundant.

Little River Lumber Co. logged this region. At one point on the trail is the "Y" where the logging train turned. And you can see the shallow remains of an old log slide road.

FIGHTING CREEK NATURE TRAIL
About 1.0 mile roundtrip

Here is a pleasant walk in the park for those who come to the Sugarlands Visitor Center, near Park Headquarters, and have only a little time to spend. The trail circles through mixed woodland, crosses little Fighting Creek and passes a cabin made of logs. It starts a few yards from Sugarlands Visitor Center, at the intersection of Little River and Newfound Gap Roads.

NOAH "BUD" OGLE NATURE TRAIL
About 0.75 mile roundtrip

A profusion of wildflowers, with especially good stands of large white trillium and white clintonia, makes this one of the three best nature trails for a springtime walk. The old log home and an old-time tub mill, powered by water from a mountain stream, offer a charming and authentic look back into the early history of mountain people. The trail loops off the Cherokee Orchard Road. It is not far from the heart of Gatlinburg.

SMOKEMONT NATURE TRAIL
0.75 mile roundtrip

This trail, which loops off the Smokemont Campground road, is an area that was logged until the late 1920's. So it offers a good look at natural reforestation.

You can stand in one place on the trail and see 17 tree species. An added attraction on this trail is that it crosses Bradley Fork Creek, a typical swift, clear mountain stream, rushing along a creekbed strewn with boulders.

SPRUCE-FIR NATURE TRAIL
0.5 mile roundtrip

Walk this trail in July and August and find the coolness of May. You'll also find the flora of Canada—old-growth spruce and fir trees and other plants as much at home far to the North. Some of the biggest trees started growing before the American Revolution. Their roots are nourished by the moist remains of their ancestors.

Notice the rotting moss-covered logs. Notice other slight mounds where older logs are almost part of the soil again. Though this site is more sheltered than the crest of the mountains, high winds blow down these trees. Winter often loads the trees with ice and snow, making the work of the winds easier. Also making it easier are the shallow root systems of spruce and fir. They have no tap roots. Notice some trees that appear to stand on their roots. This came about because these trees started growing as seedlings on the moist trunks of decaying fallen trees. When decay was complete, the new trees were left standing on their "prop" roots.

The entrance-exit for the circular trail is from the south side of the Clingmans Dome Road, about 2.7 miles west of that road's intersection with the Newfound Gap Road and about 4.3 miles east of the Clingmans Dome Parking Area. Only eastbound traffic is supposed to stop at the small parking area at the trailhead.

Trail elevation is a little less than 6,000 feet.

SUGARLANDS VALLEY ALL-ACCESS NATURE TRAIL
0.5 mile roundtrip

This paved, wheelchair and stroller accessible loop trail starts off Newfound Gap Road (U.S. 441) just a half mile south of Sugarlands

Visitor Center. It features some wonderful exhibits along the way that explain the area's natural and cultural history. Other highlights include old homesites, boulders, and a large mountain stream (the West Prong of the Little Pigeon River).

TRAIL INDEX

PHOTO CREDITS